D1515708

The Delicate Dance

Living White Being Black: A Memoir

by

Paula Heariold-Kinney

DORRANCE
PUBLISHING CO
EST. 1920
PITTSBURGH, PENNSYLVANIA 15238

Dorrance Publishing Co
585 Alpha Drive
Suite 103
Pittsburgh, PA 15238
Visit our website at www.dorrancebookstore.com

ISBN: 978-1-6470-2290-7
eISBN: 978-1-6470-2856-5

This memoir was written for all who have delicately danced to keep in step with the steady cadence of the music

Dedicated to Daddy, Mama, and Miss Grace

We don't see things the way they are;
we see things the way we are.
The Talmud

"Racism is pervasive. My blackness is not something that can be ignored. I have to get it out of the way, before evidence of my expertise is valued."

First Awareness

"Get away from my daughter, you dirty little nigger girl!" That screeching scream was directed at me. The sound of the woman's piercing voice still resonates in my head. The frightened look on her daughter's face, as she looked over at me, continues to haunt me. I was four years old when this incident took place. It was the first time that I learned that there was an invisible boundary between the little white girl and myself, based on the color of my skin.

On the day of this incident, I began the morning by excitedly accompanying my mother to pick up my sisters' and my new clothes that my mother ordered from the Sears & Roebuck catalog. When we arrived at Sears, there were several women lined up in two parallel lines, waiting for their purchases. Directly across from my mother and me was a woman with a little girl who looked to be about my same age. She had long straight blonde hair, wore a lavender frilly dress, and had on shiny black patent-leather shoes. We both gazed at each other, giggling shyly. I walked slowly toward the little girl and took her hand. That's when her mother hurled the horrific racial slurs at me. My mother, who had not realized what had happened, embarrassingly, quickly came over. She placed her arm around my shoulders, while walking me back where we were standing in line. Tears flowed down my face; I looked across at the little girl, who was no longer smiling. I was confused and scared, believing I had done something wrong. Without saying a word, my mother continued to stand in line, looking straight ahead, with her arm still around my shoulders.

Mama was a stately, beautiful tall woman. Her smooth skin was as light as that of the white lady who snatched her little girl away from me. Mama had brown soft curly hair, and Caucasian features. She was adopted as an infant and knew nothing about her ethnic background, nor did she care to know. She considered herself black and resented whenever anyone referred to her as white. She was very protective of any person who treated our family disrespectful because of the color of our skin. She was especially protected of me, being the youngest child.

Mama and me. My consummate protector.

On our way home, my mother tried to console me by saying, "That lady was not nice and the things she said about you were untrue. Some people are just mean!" Mama's comments did not help me. The hurtful and racist remarks the lady hurled toward me at the department store caused me to see myself as an ugly little black girl, with nappy hair, unlike the way I saw the little white girl, as pretty with silky straight blonde hair. Before this distinct situation, I had not viewed myself in such a repellant manner.

Racial disparities were pervasive in Des Moines, Iowa, during the 40s and 50s. There was a relatively small population of blacks living in the city. Blacks did not migrate to Des Moines until the 1920s. Many were very submissive toward whites, fearing that if they were not, they could be in jeopardy of losing their jobs, or not being employed at all. There were few blacks that had formal education, which relegated them to jobs requiring little skills, such as domestic work. Black men especially were adversely affected during these times, finding little work or being hired in jobs that offered meager pay. The ability for men to provide for their family with necessities was difficult. Many black women became the primary "breadwinner," which stripped men of their manhood. Both black men and women learned to adapt, behave, and conform, in accordance with what whites expected of them, which was to show respect by placating them in ways that made whites feel comfortable and in control.

I was born, during that era, in Des Moines, Iowa, on November 18th, 1945, to Dorothea and Eugene Frazier. They divorced after a seven-year marriage due to Eugene's alcoholism. My mother married George Heariold. My mother brought three girls into their marriage: Connie, Judy, and me (Paula). George brought two of his girls into their marriage, Mary, whom we called "Beannie," and Barbara. Together they had a blended family of five girls. George was smitten by my mother the moment he laid eyes on her, and cherished her girls, as though they were his biological daughters. My mother felt the same way about George's daughters. I never thought of my sisters as stepsisters; they were just my sisters. After four years of marriage, George and Dorothea gave birth to two daughters: Kathy and Dorothy. I was pretty much the "baby" until Kathy was born four years later, which is why I believe I was so close to my father. Everyone said I looked like Daddy. We formed a very special bond until the day he died.

We were fortunate to retain ownership of our home; few black families were not financially able to purchase their own homes. We lived in a three-bedroom stucco house, with one bathroom. Having one bathroom made it burdensome for my father to compete with seven women in the house. My sisters and I slept in two of the bedrooms; one room had three twin beds, and the other two twin beds. We never minded sharing a bed with one of the other sisters. I was proud of our home, and the house still sits on the corner where I spent most of my life growing up, until I graduated from college. The memories of living there are as fresh today as they were then.

I grew up believing that we were not poor, but knew that my parents struggled financially. I knew that some families struggled more than we did. Black families in our "class" looked out for one another. I recall one of my Mother's friends, Miss Babs, received food from the government. I remember seeing everything she shared with our family was stamped with BIG red letters printed on each box, "U.S. Government." I loved the cheese which made the best grilled cheese sandwich; however, I detested the spam, which Mama fried frequently for dinner. The worst was the powdered milk! We did not quality to receive the government food because our income was "too high". "I would have been too embarrassed to have the boxes of free food be delivered to our house. When I shared these feelings with my mother she said, "I never want you to be too embarrassed for what God has provided and to be thankful that our neighbors were so kind to share their blessings with us."

The older sisters had very close relationships, as well as the two younger sisters, who spent time playing together. Because of the age differences between my older and younger sisters; as a middle child, I became pretty independent and self-directed. I spent time reading Nancy Drew books and playing dress-up in Mama's high-heeled shoes and jewelry. Many times, I was in my own imaginary world, pretending I was a famous actress or dancer. I was very comfortable being by myself, not ever feeling left out or alone. Without guidance from my parents, regarding the shaping of my future endeavors, I spent my life making my own decisions about the direction I wanted to go. However, my parents modeled the values and virtues that shaped me. They also taught me that most people are well meaning and gracious. I found this to be true along my journey. My mother bestowed a quality of trust before she passed judgment on others. I was fortunate to possess this same trait.

Acculturation

Just as their elders taught my parents, about behaviors that were essential for assimilating into a white culture, Mama and Daddy taught us the same principles. They drilled the same mantra into my sisters and me. We were instructed to act very polite and to always use proper diction. They said, "Do not speak or laugh too loudly. Use correct grammar. Do not let 'them' know our business, respect your teachers, and never get into trouble at school." We repeatedly heard these rules more than once and adhered to our parents' expectations, seldom veering off track.

Our family juggled between two worlds: black at home, where we were relaxed and uninhibited or while visiting relatives and friends, and switched our behavior around whites, using soft voices and muffled laughter. We made sure to always be on our best behavior and to respond respectfully, even though we may not have been treated with the same respect. I learned at a very early age the importance of changing behaviors and taking on distinctive traits of changing my personality; depending on which environment I entered. I practiced the "drill" so well that I, seamlessly, would speak with perfect diction. Sometimes my black friends would ask irritably, "Why are you talking like a white person?" I didn't think I was talking like a white person; my way of speaking became natural to me. However, when I was solely with black friends, I automatically began speaking in a black dialogue, raising the range of my voice and unconsciously using incorrect subject-verb agreements. My laughter also became more rambunctious. My black friends and I talked at high voice levels, speaking at the same time, constantly interrupting each other, and laughed jovially. I was amused when Carolyn, who was my roommate and is not black, said to me recently, "I remember one time when your black friends came to visit at our apartment how surprised I was that you didn't sound like the same person." She said she was in her bedroom and felt a little uncomfortable joining us because we seemed to have such a close kinship. She told me, "I was not sure if I would be intruding." I was amazed that Carolyn shared this with me because I was not aware that I had automatically switched my dialect to a black brogue. Switching dialect just became natural.

While still wanting to preserve my black heritage, yet fit in with the Eurocentric culture, I learned to acculturate between two cultures. Admittedly, I enjoyed, purposely, switching dialects around white colleagues, who directly reported to me. I believe by doing so, we developed a certain bond. For instance, in my role as a high school principal, it was fun using my black dialect with my secretary and my other administrative team, who were white. For example, my secretary would come in and say to me, while shaking her index finger, "Girl (emphasis on the word "girl"), you will never believe what just happened!" We both would affectionately laugh. In a leadership role, I was able to have fun with my immediate staff. They observed my need to "switch" when I was in my "professional" role. However, I would never have used a black dialect in a formal setting, even in front of the teachers I supervised, believing I would not be taken seriously, or judged that I was using improper grammar. I was very cautious with whom I shared my lighthearted black side while I was at work.

Hues of Color

Since Biblical times the variances of skin color often determined one's ranking status. I continue to observe this phenomenon, not only in the United States but also in my travels to countries inhabited by the majority of people with dark skin. The lighter the person's skin, generally, the more prominent positions they held. Skin color may be a determining factor of how a black person is treated, not only by whites but also by other blacks. Black people with very dark skin may appear frightening to some white people, especially black males with dark skin. I imagine the reason is that black males have been perceived to be dangerous or a threat. If a white person, male or female, is walking down the street alone and a black male is walking behind him, the white person's antenna goes up, believing he may be in harm's way. Several whites have shared with me that this fear factor, unfortunately, is true.

Lighter-skinned blacks appear more acceptable by whites. Some blacks look at lighter-skinned blacks as being prettier or more handsome. Some blacks might treat a light-skinned person unkind, by assuming the light-skinned person believes he or she is better than the darker-skinned person. When I was a teenager, I recall my friends commenting about my lighter-skinned sister, "Girl, your sister is so pretty. She looks like a white girl." Ironically, like my mother, my sister did not view this as a compliment. I also recall when I was younger, female girls, including some of my relatives, emphatically stating, "When I get married, I'm going to marry a light-skinned boy with straight hair. I don't want my kids to be dark with nappy hair!" I believe many black guys felt the same way about dating a dark-skinned girl, even if the guy himself had dark skin. As a young girl, I had wished that my skin were lighter. This stereotype, about having lighter skin as being prettier or more handsome, currently continues to exists in the minds of many, by both blacks and whites.

Insecurities about how I might be judged, as a black person, were often at the forefront of my thinking when I interviewed for a job or was invited to participate in a group where I was the only black person. I worked at ameliorating any negative feelings that I thought might have been surfacing in the minds of others. I often would exhibit overtly professional mannerisms and an overly gregarious personality. I barely could focus on questions being asked of me because of hearing the voices in my head saying, "Paula, chill and relax. Why are you allowing yourself to become so anxious?" I could feel my smile getting frozen and my eyes twitching. There are still occasions when I enter an all-white environment when I want to say, "Okay, now that you see that I am black, let's move on." These emotions, I recognize, are my own personal feelings of angst, and may have had little to do with what the people in the room are thinking. I realize these messages in my head may have more to do with my insecurities about being "the only," as well as, the negative experiences I encountered in my past.

My sisters and I reinforced each other's negative feelings about each other. We compared our skin color by holding one arm up against the other. We would say, "You are darker than I am." We had been indoctrinated and conditioned to believe that dark skin was a negative characteristic to possess. I continue to work at not carrying that belief about others and myself. I personally observed, when I was a teacher and school administrator, how lighter students were given more attention and treated more kindly by teachers than the way darker-skinned children were treated. White students and light-skinned black students seemed to receive more positive attention and be given more patience with discipline. Black kids would come to me and say, "That mean teacher doesn't like me!" I understood completely what the student was conveying to me. What I heard from his hurt feelings was, "The teacher doesn't value me as a person." I had experienced the same perception, as a child, when I was in school. I felt the same way when Mr. Wilson, the band teacher, made me sit in the back row in the band room. Real or unreal, it's a hurtful feeling.

My white friends were curious about the different shades of colors among my sisters and me. They asked questions such as, "Why do some of your sisters have light skin and others dark skin?" Or they might ask, "Is that your real sister?" Our contrasting skin colors became a topic that came up frequently. My sister, Connie, was very light skinned with freckles; Judy had a bronze complexion; Beanie's skin tone was ebony; Barbara's was tannish, and mine was chocolate brown. Both Kathy and Dorothy Ann's skin color was as light as my mother's.

Hues of Color

Sadly, on more than one occasion, we would make negative remarks about each other's skin color. Once when my older sisters were angry with Connie, they chased her around the house mimicking an Indian dance as they repeatedly sang, "We eat white meat." On another occasion, when I made my sisters angry, I became the target of their verbal abuse when they called me "little ugly darkie." My mother got very upset with us when she heard us flung these verbal attacks at each other. She admonished us saying, "I told you girls, more than once, that I will not allow you to talk to each other with cruel and hurtful remarks about your skin colors." She told us that we all had beautiful skin tones. Mama had been the target of bullying when she was in school; black kids accused her of trying to be white, and white kids accused her of acting too black.

I believe variations in skin tones among people of color will always be an emerging topic, not just by whites, but also by blacks. It seems to be a human curiosity, as well as an unjust way to discriminate. Ironically, many of my white friends lie in the sun to get tan. I remember my college friends asking me as we were lying on the beach, "Paula, do you ever get sunburned?" My resounding answer was, "Yes, and it hurts as badly as it hurts you." They were always surprised when I pulled down my swimming suit straps to show them that I also had tan marks. I have pondered often about why skin color is such a focus of concern when it seems so absurd. I have come to the realization that I will never have the answer, while still realizing the color issue will continue to be a predictor on how one may be judged.

Riveting Impressions

I learned from both parents the importance of having a superior work ethic, regardless of whether I enjoyed my job. My father said, "Work as hard as you would as if you own the company." He also said, empathically, "Life isn't always easy or fair, but that there are payoffs for sticking things out, without comprising principles." Both parents were hard workers without complaining about their jobs. Perhaps they knew it was what they had to do in order to take care of seven girls, or maybe they just didn't mind working.

My mother cleaned houses for some very nice families. On occasion, I went with Mama to homes where she worked. I dreamed that one day I might live in such beautiful homes. The homes seemed gigantic to me. I was amazed that they always had so much food in their refrigerators; some even had freezers stocked with frozen pizzas and ice cream. The nice ladies always offered me to take whatever I wanted, which politely, I refused. I knew Mama would not have been happy with me if I accepted. One thing I found astonishing was, the ladies Mama worked for spent more time talking and drinking coffee with her than my mother spent cleaning their homes. They said to my mother, "Dorothea, you can clean this room or that room the next time you come to work." I witnessed that the ladies really enjoyed my mother's company, as much as having her clean their houses. I relished watching my mother's ease at interacting with these ladies. My mother, seamlessly, could engage with most people she met even if it was the first time she met them. She was a master at making people feel comfortable, regardless of whom they were.

Being aware of my dark skin I became visibly mindful, when my mother was talking to her employers, that Mama was as light skinned as they were. I began to contemplate if the ladies noticed the stark difference between my mother's light skin color and Caucasian features that differed from my dark skin and Negroid features. Once when I left work with Mama I asked, "Do you think the ladies you work for think that I am adopted?" I recall my mother stopping, as we walked to the bus stop, looking surprised by my question, "Why would you say such a ridiculous thing?" I didn't say anything about skin color or how we looked different. I just replied, "Just because." Mama looked at me perplexed, "You are being silly." I didn't think I was being silly. I had an uneasy feeling and could tell that Mama was uncomfortable wanting to pursue the conversation so I let it drop. I never brought it up again.

My father worked at a car dealership. His boss, Mr. Manning, owned Paul Manning's Chevrolet. Daddy was the only black employee and prided himself on working hard. He was a self-made mechanic. He was really proud of his job. I loved seeing him leave the house in the morning wearing his crisp white uniform, carrying his black lunch bucket, as he flashed his big dimpled smile. He always kissed my mother goodbye before he left for work. Even as a little girl, there was a sadness that came over me when Daddy walked out the door. I knew it was not an easy job, not because of the hard labor, because my father did not mind hard work. I knew he would be entering an environment of consternation, one in which he needed to walk a fine line of being friendly and working hard, yet staying in his "place," ensuring to appeal to the sensibilities of his boss and coworkers. I overheard Daddy talking to my mother about how he had to eat lunch alone because he was not invited to join his coworkers. He shared how unfriendly some of the other workers were, including laughing and telling racial jokes in front of him. He said he mostly stayed to himself and just did his work, knowing he was not at liberty to respond negatively to these remarks so as not to put his job in jeopardy. He shared these remarks with my mother, not as a complaint, but more about expressing that this was just common behavior among some of the white guys. Even though he liked his job, the tension was visible on my father's face when he came home from work, having to endure unkind remarks from some of the other workers. My sisters and I knew to give Daddy his space and not to talk to him until he had time to read the paper and relax. The weekends were always much more at ease and casual at our home. There was laughter, joking, and music playing throughout the house. I cherished our weekends together.

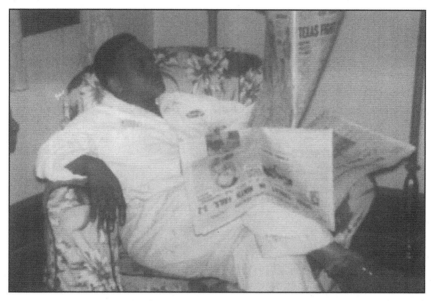

Daddy relaxing after work.

I especially looked forward to seeing my father have fun with his buddies, with whom he had known most of his life. They came over to our house every Friday evening after they all got off from work. The guys, who all were given silly nicknames by each other, names like Horse Collar, Collie, and Booker. They sat on the steps of our front porch, passed around a pint of Jim Beam whiskey, which they all took a sip from. I loved their thunderous laughter and the way they teased each other by telling made up fibs about what each one did or did not do. They were at ease and had so much fun, which was the complete opposite of the tensed way Daddy was when he came home from work during the weekdays. When the "fellas" left our house, my dad drove our family to the Rock Island Train Station, where my dad "Red Capped" on Sunday nights. He would buy us the best "10 hamburgers for $5 Special." We waited in the car while Daddy picked up the hamburgers. He knew some of the other guys who worked at the station, both white and black. They would always come over to the car to say hello to us, while we were eating. Daddy had a friendly connection and relationship with his coworkers at the railroad station. He seemed to enjoy the atmosphere at the train station much more than he did at the car dealership. I loved our Friday night tradition, especially watching Daddy genuinely laugh and interact with "the guys."

On Saturday nights, when my sisters and I were supposed to be in bed sleeping, my mom and dad picked out some of their favorite 45 records, which consisted of mostly blues to play on the record player. My sisters and I sneaked out of bed and sat on the upstairs steps so we could spy on my parents dancing together. While they swayed together to the music, it seemed to soothe their souls. They looked so romantic together. My mother's soft dark curly brown waves bounced in step with the music. Her light brown eyes were fixated on Daddy. Daddy seemed to look as handsome as ever. His skin was a reddish brown and he had beautiful gray-blue eyes. He had a strong defined jaw and muscular arms. He was a strikingly colossal man. My sisters and I were mesmerized with the love our parents showed toward one another.

When I expressed the love that I embraced regarding these family reflections with some of my friends, I am not sure they understood how impactful these memories were to me. My memories were impactful because I was able to keep my focus on the happy times, rather than think about the struggles and uphill battles my parents fought to make ends meet; not to mention the insidious cloud of racism that prevailed. I remember one of my friends inquiring, "Didn't it seem weird to sit in a dark car at a train station eating hamburgers?" I was lost for words, realizing it was inconceivable for my friend to understand the jubilant feelings of joy I received during these special moments I shared with my family.

Sunday Morning Church

Attending Union Baptist Church filled my heart with elation. Still today when I attend a black Baptist church, it is one of the ultimate black experiences that keep me connected with my African American heritage. I become emotionally steeped into my culture while singing and rocking to gospel music. I also value listening to the congregation respond, in union, to the preacher as he preaches his sermon. The black church keeps me from venturing too far from my upbringing. When our children were young, my husband and I made an effort to take them to a traditional black church, believing this would expose them to a rich and genuine African American experience, as well as help them feel a linkage with the black side of their birthroots.

Every Sunday morning, I woke up to my mother playing uplifting gospel music. It was so emotional and moving. I especially loved listening to Mahalia Jackson, who had a powerful and heavenly voice. My sisters and I scrambled to get ready for church. My mother continued to call and warn us, "You're going to get left behind if you are not in the car within the next two minutes!" The majority of the black people in Des Moines attended Union Baptist Church. The only exception was the few black professionals who attended the African American Episcopal Church, which I thought was way too "uppity" and staid for me. The members of this congregation sang old Negro hymnals out of the books that were placed in the small compartments in front of the pews. The people who attended the African American Episcopal Church were the few blacks in the community who came from a lineage of college graduates.

They "pledged" to fraternities and sororities and were invited to be members of a club called the *Links*, a club for college-graduated black women. Their children belonged to a prestigious club called *Jack and Jill*, where the children were taught "proper" etiquette. Upon graduating from high school, the *Jack and Jill* members attended a Cotillion Ball where the teenagers were "presented" to the black upper-middle-class society. The girls wore elaborate white formals and the guys wore white tuxedos. I never aspired to be connected with this group of snobbery. Too be honest, my parents didn't fit the mold of this bourgeois class of black people. It amused me when Daddy said, with a hearty laugh, "Shoot, it don't matter how many degrees and clubs they belong, they still just black folk in the eyes of the white people. It ain't going to help them get treated any better!" Even though I didn't aspire to belong to these clubs, I didn't feel as strongly as Daddy did by judging what clubs others wanted to belong. In fact, many of these people were trailblazers and leaders in our community. They opened doors for other black people. Some were teachers or doctors; however, many worked in low-ranking jobs such as elevator operators, at high-end department stores, or they were hotel greeters who wore formal red uniforms with shiny brass buttons and wore white gloves.

Conversely, at Union Baptist Church, the people were very down to earth and unpretentious. The congregation sang old spiritual gospel music, songs that had been passed down from generation to generation. Most of the people knew each other, even those that lived in different parts of the city. The women wore big distinctly shaped hats in different sizes and vibrant colors. Looking down at the pews, from the back of the church, I could see a rainbow of colors that looked to me like a cluster of multicolored bouquets of flowers. My sisters and I were also dressed up; I felt proud to wear my shiny black patent-leather shoes, which reminded me of how pretty I thought the shoes were when I first saw them on the little girl, who was wearing them at Sears Department Store. I had long tried not to associate the pretty patent-leather shoes with the hurtful incident caused by the rude white lady who became so hysterical when I took her daughter's hand.

The women at the church greeted each other with hugs, wide smiles, and laughter, asking each other, "Girl, what you been up to?" The men were all showcasing their dapper well-tailored double-breasted suits, crispy white starched shirts, wide colorful ties, and wore fedora hats. There was not a man in the group whose shoes were not beautifully buffed and shined "to the hills."

The men slapped each other on the back and talked and laughed rowdily and good-naturedly. They were able to let go of any stress and enjoy every moment of their blackness. The men were among family and friends where there was no need to adhere to the conduct of behaviors expected of them in front of white people. It was obvious they were feeling proud.

The church service lasted at least two hours, depending on how emotionally stirred the churchwomen got. Just when it seemed that the service was almost over, the men and women would shout, "Preach it Pastor!" The preacher would start preaching all over again and the music and choir would begin singing. Sometimes the women would start dancing all over the church and the ushers would try to calm them down by running after them, while trying to fan them at the same time. My sisters and I would start snickering and my mother would give us the "evil eye." We knew to look straight ahead and try as hard as we could to look as though we were earnestly focused on the church service. I tried hard to think of other things and drew pictures on the offering envelopes to help make the time go by.

After the service, all the adults congregated outside the church. They wanted to savor each moment of connecting with friends, those with whom they may not see again until the following Sunday. I remember several of Mama's friends coming up to me saying, "Come here, Paula Marie. Give me some sugar." I didn't want to be rude so I waited until they weren't looking and then wiped the lipstick off my cheeks."

After church, our family sat at the dining room table and ate Mama's delicious fried chicken she had prepared early that morning, which stayed warm in the oven. We always had mashed potatoes, gravy, and corn or peas with the chicken. On Sunday evenings, we had a light dinner; usually macaroni and cheese, or everyone helped themself to whatever leftovers were still in the refrigerator. As I think back, it amazes me how one chicken fed our entire family. My mother could cut the big fat chicken in several smaller pieces, with the exception of the legs, which we had to take turns having. I remember the arguments my sisters and I had over who was going to get which piece of the chicken. I would whine, "Barbara got a leg last time! " Daddy always got the breast.

The highlight of my Sunday evening was sitting down on the floor, while my parents sat on the couch. We watched *Lassie* and *The Ed Sullivan Show*. We ate Oreo cookies and vanilla ice cream. Sunday's were pretty special at the Heariold home.

Self-Sacrifices

As I grew older, I became more aware of the many constraints placed on my parents. They provided us with nice, albeit, inexpensive clothes and made sure we looked neat and clean. My parents never allowed us to complain about what we didn't have; always teaching us to be grateful for what we had. They taught us to be kind to people, regardless of one's ethnicity. It was sometimes difficult for me to "fake" that I liked people with whom I believed treated my family unjust. I can still recall that there were establishments where we knew we were not welcome to eat. I could tell by the negative looks we got when we went to certain places. On one occasion, my mother and I sat at the food counter to buy a cherry coke at Woolworths's. Des Moines was not supposed to be segregated; however, there were subliminal ways that blacks were treated that felt otherwise. When my mother and I sat for many minutes waiting to be served, the server stood right in front of us, looking in the opposite direction, as though we were not supposed to be seated at the counter. We were not served until Mama stated firmly, "My daughter and I would like to buy a cherry coke." The man, who looked at us with disgust, slammed down the two drinks, without saying a word. While we were drinking our Cokes, Mama prompted the rude man to engage in a conversation, she said, "So how is your day going?" Shocked by her question, he replied dryly, "Fine. And how is your day going?" Before I knew it, my mother and the man were talking about how they both graduated from East High School. We left the counter with the man saying to my mother, "Y'all come back." My mother easily could make friends out of the "unfriendly. She loved people unconditionally. I believed I followed in her steps, believing that seemly unkind people are basically good, once you get to know them.

There were hurtful situations my parents encountered. My father was denied the opportunity to purchase several homes as he was exploring to buy a new home. He was proud that he had saved enough money to buy his family a bigger house. When he saw a home he liked, he went to the real estate office to speak with the realtor. He was told the house had been sold, although it remained on the market for several months. I was consciously aware of how hurt my parents felt when they were faced with such encounters. I still recall my parents' wounded looks, yet, I knew there was no recourse, during that time, for dealing with the acts of injustice, which made these situations all the more disheartening. My father continued looking for a home they could purchase in a modest neighborhood but, after getting discouraged, decided to remain where we lived and remodeled our small kitchen and dining room. After the remodel, I felt as though we lived in a mansion.

Treasured Holidays

In spite of the hardships that my parents faced, their commitment to making our holidays extraordinary was indisputable. I still reminisce about all the good times we shared with family and friends, celebrating our holidays.

Thanksgiving was invariably exceptional. The aroma of the turkey permeated throughout our home. My mother put the turkey in the oven overnight; the savory smell hit our nose the moment we awakened. We dressed up for Thanksgiving as if we were going to church, even though we never left home. I always helped set the table eloquently, pretending I lived in one of the pretty houses where Mama worked. We held hands and said a Thanksgiving prayer before we ate. The dinner was scrumptious. Everyone stuffed themselves with the traditional black Thanksgiving dinner of dressing, sweet potatoes, macaroni and cheese, collard greens, pumpkin pie and Grandma Brown's steaming homemade dinner rolls. Our wooden dining room table was covered with an embroidered white tablecloth my Grandma Brown had passed down to Mama. We didn't have matching chairs, but enough chairs to seat the nine of us around the table, plus, if needed, we squeezed card table chairs in to accommodate the extra guests Mama might have invited, usually college students, that didn't have a place to eat on Thanksgiving Day. One thing for sure, we always had enough food!

Thanksgiving was fantastic, but Christmas was really extraordinary. We always attended Christmas Eve Services. Afterwards, we sat by the Christmas tree, drank homemade eggnog, ate hot chili, and listened to Christmas music.

A few days before Christmas Day, Daddy drove us around every year to see all the decorated homes where the wealthy white people lived. Although, I thought the decorations were pretty; even as a young child, I felt resentment that our family could not live in a big pretty house in a pristine neighborhood. Regardless of my feelings, my sisters and I were still in awe as we passed by and looked at each of the homes.. However, I loved our decorations just as much as the rich people's houses. There was something unique about having our very own Christmas decorations. We always had a small but decorated tree with colorful bulbs that flashed off and on, and silver stencils were strategically placed all around our tree. My sisters and I could hardly wait to go to bed so that we could wake up early in the morning to see what Santa brought. My parents started playing Christmas music around 5:00 A.M., alerting us that it was time to come downstairs. Placed around the Christmas tree was one big special unwrapped gift for each of us, like a big doll or bicycle that we had re-quested for Santa to bring. The dolls that we received were always white. Even as a little girl I wondered why none of the dolls had brown skin. Strangely, I never stopped to ask; I guess I assumed that was just the way dolls were sup-posed to look.

Look what Santa brought me

White dolls for Christmas

One year I asked Santa for a pogo stick. I was so excited when I found out he had left one for me. My sisters were annoyed with me as I hopped all around the house the entire day. What I did not expect for Christmas, but also wanted from Santa, was a shiny new tricycle. I could not believe my eyes when I saw it. My parents, on many occasions, would surprise us with a big gift that we didn't request. In addition, there were several smaller wrapped presents that usually contained such gifts as colorful winter gloves with matching wool scarves, or underwear. We weren't as enthralled with the smaller gifts, but always told our parents how much we liked them. Daddy gave each of us ten dollars, a few days before Christmas, so we had money to buy a gift for each of our parents. I loved taking the bus to Woolworth's with my sisters to pick out gifts for Daddy and Mama. Our parents made a big deal over each of the individual gifts my sisters and I gave to them. I bought Daddy Old Spice cologne every single year. We usually spent the Christmas day lounging around the house and playing with our toys. Several of my parents' friends came by our house to say "Merry Christmas" and to toast a small glass of Mogen David wine. No one knocked on the door, friends just walked in and out of our house throughout the day. One of my vivid memories was listening to the Christmas songs that played throughout Christmas Day, songs that were sung by Elvis Priestley, Johnny Mathis, and Nat King Cole. To this day, I still play their Christmas songs during the Christmas holiday.

Easter Sunday was another special day. Our parents always bought us new clothes, which included frilly white gloves and Easter bonnets. I always requested new shiny black patent leather shoes. When we woke up on Easter Morning, we received Easter baskets filled with different colored jellybeans and spongy yellow marshmallow candy chickens and rabbits. I recall one year my father even bought us two live blue and pink dyed chickens. The poor chickens seldom lived very long, which made me sad. At the time, my parents believed it was a special Easter gift, but became aware of how inhumane it was and stopped buying us the live dyed colored chickens. Although, I generally complained about having to go to the beauty shop, this was one of those times I didn't mind going, because I loved having my hair pressed and styled in flowing curls for Easter. I will always remember the sacrifices my parents made to ensure we had magnificent holidays. I have tried to recreate the same traditions for my family; however, I don't believe I will ever be able to recreate the holidays that my parents provided for my sisters and me.

All dressed up for Easter with curled hair.

Vacation Time

The annual summer drive to Los Angeles, on Route 66, to visit my Aunt Louise was tortuous; Daddy would seldom stop the car. When we passed by a Dairy Queen restaurant, we begged for him to stop so we could get an ice cream cone. His remark was, "Your mother has prepared enough food." My mother made a big basket of fried chicken and loads of bologna sandwiches, on white bread, with globs of mayonnaise. She included Hostess Cupcakes and Ding Dongs, which she purchased at the discount bakery. For our drinks, she filled two thermo jugs of very sweet grape and orange Kool-Aid. Both parents and all seven sisters were piled together in our 1953 Chevrolet station wagon, with no air-conditioning in 90-plus-degree temperatures. My father had the trip mapped out so that he would only stop when necessary, for gas and for us to use the restroom at truck stops. Blacks were not allowed to use the restrooms at restaurants or stay at any of the motels. We slept in the car at night. My sisters and I were supposed to remain very quiet so Daddy could sleep and be rested before he continued to drive. However, we would pinch and kick each other, continuously saying, "Move over! I don't have any room." Or, "If you don't stop it, I am going to wake up Daddy and tell on you." Mama would look back at us and say, "You kids better knock it off." This was ongoing grumbling that continued throughout our trip. My father would wake up and threaten to leave us on the side of the road. I actually thought he might carry out his threat if we didn't behave.

As we drove by several hotels, I used to think about what it would be like if we were rich, like white people. I believed that all white people were rich.

Later in life, many of my white friends shared with me that they had many of the same experiences on their long car trips. The only exception was they had the privilege of stopping at Motel 6 so they could sleep at night. I used to close my eyes on those long road trips and imagine stopping at one of the big hotels, having someone hold the door open and say, "Welcome to Holiday Inn."

On one of our visits to Los Angeles, while my parents were laughing and reminiscing with Aunt Louise and my sisters were playing outside, I decided to lie down on Aunt Louise's bed to watch television on her tiny black-and-white television. Billy Graham, the famous evangelist, happened to be on television. I had watched Dr. Graham preach previously when Mama watched him on television at our home. Mama always had tears flowing down her face when Dr. Graham invited people to move from the pew and walk down to the front of the church to accept Jesus Christ as their Savior. My mother was such a strong follower of Christ; I was moved by her faith. When I heard Dr. Graham extend an invitation to accept Christ and saw so many people walking up to Dr. Graham, I got off the bed and walked over to the television, knelt down on my knees, and accepted Christ. I was eight years old. Seeing so many people of all colors accept Christ, I realized that Christ loves all people. Unfortunately, I found that Dr. Graham was not the most accepting person toward all people. However, I still give him credit for encouraging many people to know Christ, which is most important.

My other unforgettable memory was my visits to my aunts who lived in Keysville, Missouri. Almost every summer, Daddy would drive my sisters and me to visit Aunt Frances and Aunt Lillie Ann. They were my dad's mother's sisters. Daddy would drive us there and return a couple of weeks later to pick us up. I am sure my parents savored the quietness of having us gone for a couple of weeks. I really enjoyed going to visit my aunts; it was such a different environment than Des Moines. Everyone lived on a farm and drove on dirt roads. For some reason, as a child, this really intrigued me. I especially liked playing with my cousin, who actually was my stepsister, Little Francis. She lived with Aunt Francis. Little Francis was adopted because Daddy's first wife deserted their children while he was in the service (too long of a story to include). I was about nine years old when I would go to visit. Little Francis was only a couple years older than I. My aunts lived directly across the dirt road from each other. I thought it was hysterical how they yelled from each other's houses to talk to each other, instead of just walking over to the other's home. They would yell,

"Louise! Will the girls be eating at your house tonight?" The response, "Frances, it don't matter to me." They talked to each other in this method throughout the day. However, there were two things I didn't like about going to visit, one was going to the outhouse to use the bathroom. I always held my nose and tried desperately not to breathe because of the stench that hit me in the face when I opened the wooden door. The second thing was watching Aunt Frances wring the chicken's neck in circles until the head flew off. Aunt Frances fried the chicken for dinner that same evening, extoling how fresh it was. However, it was difficult for me to eat the fried chicken after watching how the poor thing died.

I loved going to the Saturday matinees in Keysville. I found it to be so quirky. The movie theater was this small little unique building that sat on a deserted dusty road. Even though it was a segregated theater, there was something about it being so different and dorky that fascinated me. Weirdly, I wasn't even offended by the way the black kids were treated, maybe because it seemed almost ordinary for a place like Keysville. We had to stand in a separate line and were not able to buy our tickets until all the white kids bought theirs. It was also peculiar where the black kids had to sit; we had to sit upstairs in the balcony. I actually liked sitting in the balcony because I had a better view than if I sat downstairs. I was short and was able to see over the heads of the people downstairs. After the matinee was over, the black people could not leave the theater until all the white people exited. I still remember pulling a string to turn on the light upstairs when the movie was over. What was really interesting was that several white kids stood outside of the theater and waited for us to come out. Many of them waved and smiled at us. They didn't jeer or look angry at us. I believe they were just curious, wanting to know what we were about. I pretended that I was a celebrity and smiled and waved back at them, using the princess wave, elbow straight with only my hand going back and forth. Little Francis was horrified; she grabbed my arm and said, "Are you crazy! What are you doing? Let's get out of here before they call the Po-lice." I thought it was so funny how she said the name police, but I thought everyone spoke funny, both black and white people. I said, "They are just being nice." She rolled her eyes at me as we started running down the dusty road back home. I was so happy Little Francis didn't tell Aunt Francis what I did because she wouldn't have allowed us to go back to the matinee the next Saturday. The following Saturdays, after the matinee, the charade continued. This time the white kids were laughing good-naturedly, waving princess style along with me. Even Little Francis enjoyed our playfulness. I believe this was a way for the white kids to have fun with us, yet remembering to keep our boundaries and not interact more than what we were doing.

Our aunts also took us to the public swimming pool; there was a thick rope in the middle of the pool. Black kids were to swim on one side and white kids on the other. Sometimes just to be mischievous, I would entice Little Francis to swim underneath the ropes, without coming up for air. We would go to the other side of the pool without getting caught. We never told our aunts about this naughty little trick either; we knew they would be absolutely mortified. When I think back on our visits to Keysville, I remember no one thought it was a big deal about the separation of blacks and whites. That's just the way things were. Even as a young kid, I really didn't think much about it; however, I did think about the extended effort made to keep the black and white kids separated. Nevertheless, I can still see the cold snarled looks on the white parents' faces as they stared at Little Frances and me when they picked up their kids from the swimming pool.

I had never really interacted with many white adults, with the exception of those I met through the people my mom and dad worked for. The only other adult people I interacted with were Mr. and Mrs. Davis, our next-door neighbors. Mrs. Davis always looked rather lonely. I often would come out on our porch while Mr. and Mrs. Davis were sitting on their porch. I always tried to talk to them, "Hello, Mr. and Mrs. Davis. Are you having a good day?" She would nod her head and say, solemnly, "Yes, thank you." Mr. Davis didn't say anything. I didn't know if he was unfriendly or just didn't like to talk. The two of them sat on their front porch from morning until night. They had an adult daughter named Lorraine, whom they called Lee, but I rarely saw her. Mrs. Davis weighed about 300 pounds so I thought maybe it might have been hard for her to walk around. I remember when Mr. Davis died, my mom took over food and flowers. I don't think I saw anyone come to their house. They were the only white people who lived on our street. I often thought of what it was like for them to be the only white people left in the neighborhood. All the other white people moved out after blacks moved in. I wondered if they felt the same way blacks feel when they are the only ones who live in a white neighborhood.

My parents were only in their early thirties while they were raising seven girls. Both Daddy and Mama worked extremely hard to provide the very best home life, not wanting us to struggle as hard as they did. Daddy was very strict regarding his daughters dating boys or going to dances. I believe Daddy's strict demeanor was his way of sheltering his daughters from harm's way. My older sisters left home once they were out of high school. I don't believe Daddy's strictness forced my sisters to leave home so young; kids just seemed to leave home in the 50s. My older sisters' lives weren't the easiest. Mama had no choice but to depend on the older girls to do all the cleaning and to help take care of the younger ones. My sister, Judy, said she hated when she was assigned the job to comb my hair because it was so thick and difficult to comb. I used to yell real loud and say, "ouch you are hurting me!" Judy would then conk me on my hand and whisper, "You better shut up!" We still laugh about that today. I presume this was burdensome for teenagers. Our mother left our house early in the morning to take care of other people's children and clean their homes. She did not have time to clean her own home or get her younger children ready for school. When I was young, I resented that Mama could not stay home with us. Sometimes I would beg her, "Mama, will you please stay home today?" She would smile and hug me. "Mama has to get to work. You know I can't stay home today." All of my friends' mothers worked, so I don't know why I thought it would be any different for my mother. I always wanted the security of knowing Mama was at home, even if I was at school.

Astonishing Reality

I was so happy when I was finally old enough to go to school. My birthday was in November so I was able to start kindergarten at four years old. I remember my friend Pam and I skipping to school together, while our mothers trailed slowly behind us. They did not seem to have the same urgency as Pam and I did. To this day, I still remember the red plaid pleated skirt I wore. When we arrived at school, we were all told the name of our teachers and the classroom we would be in. I was sad that Pam was taken to a different classroom. She waved goodbye to her mother and looked back at me and smiled, very confidently. I was not feeling so confident and didn't want Mama to leave me by myself. My kindergarten teacher took my hand and assured me that my mother would come back to get me after lunch. I only went to school a half of day so I begin to relax and tell my mother goodbye. Besides, I was beginning to feel comfortable with my teacher; Miss Taylor was very pretty and young. I never thought about her being white. I thought all teachers were supposed to be white. I probably would have thought it weird if my teachers had been black. I will never forget Miss Taylor; I hugged her every day. She was so kind to me.

At first I didn't notice that there were no other kids of color in my class. For a fleeting moment, I thought about the encounter with the little white girl at the department store and how her mother reprimanded me for walking over to her and taking the little girl's hand. I reminded myself not to ever do that again. I began to feel lonely without Pam in the same room with me. I wasn't sure how I was supposed to approach the kids in my class. My fears were quickly alleviated as the teacher had all the children get in a circle and hold the hand of the person to the right side to them. When she counted to three, we all had to drop our hand and take the person's hand to the left of us. Thinking back on this exercise, I thought it was a pretty clever way for the teacher to not only teach us left from right, but also help us get acquainted with other students.

When we went out for recess, several little girls came up to play with me. This was my first experience actually playing with white children. One girl, in particular, kept talking to me. She was really nice. Her name was Charlotte. She and I vowed to be "best friends" on the first day of school. She was a cute freckle-faced girl who had red hair. Charlotte was my first white friend. I felt sorry for her because the other kids were not very kind to her. Some even mocked the way she walked and asked, "Why do you wear those weird shoes?" Charlotte walked with a limp and had to wear high-top brown shoes with braces. She had been stricken with polio when she was only three years old. I told my mother that I wanted her to buy me shoes just like Charlotte's since we were best friends. I seemed to always be enamored with shoes. I didn't want Charlotte to feel different. Mama said to me, "Charlotte has to wear those shoes to help her walk better." This made me feel really awful for Charlotte. I always made sure that I included her when we had to pick sides for sports during gym. The other kids would try to avoid picking Charlotte because she couldn't run very fast.

In first grade, Charlotte invited me to spend the night at her house. She told me that her mother said I was welcome to spend the night. When I told my mother how happy I was that I was invited to sleep over at Charlotte's, my father told my mother that he would not give permission for me to stay the night at a white family's home. He did not feel comfortable. He said to my mother, "Why would we let her sleep over at some white people's home that we know nothing about? We have no idea how they might treat her, or what goes on in that house." I felt really sad that my father disapproved because I knew it was important for Charlotte; I also thought it would be fun. After all, I had spent the night with Ginger and Janice. These were my two best friends. My parents had known their family for many years; their mothers and my mother were best friends. Ginger, Janice and I remained close, as have our children, three generations of friends. My sisters and I always referred to my parent's friends as "Uncle or Aunt." My parents taught my sisters and me that it was very rude to refer to an adult by his or her first name. I heard many white kids call adults by their first names; some even called their parents by their first names. I could never imagine calling my parents by their first names. If I did, I could hear my Daddy saying, as he rolled his eyes at me, "I hope I didn't hear you just call me George!" Sometimes I would call Daddy George when I was kidding with him. Even then, it seemed funny when I said it. After much discussion with my father, my mother convinced Daddy that he might consider allowing me to spend the night at Charlotte's. Daddy said to my mother, "Only if you make a personal visit to Charlotte's home to meet with Charlotte's mother," he added, "as well as see the living conditions." My mother and I went to Charlotte's house. The two mothers got along really well and Mama was pleased with the living environment. I was so excited when Daddy reluctantly gave his approval for me to stay all night with Charlotte.

Charlotte was an only child and had her own bedroom, with twin beds. I thought it was strange that she had two beds in her room since she was the only one who slept in her room. Beside each of the beds were two nightstands with cute lamps placed on each one. We didn't have nightstands or pretty lamps in our bedrooms. I had never heard of the term "nightstands." They just looked like little tables to me. In my bedroom we turned on the light by pulling the cord that hung next to the light in the ceiling, similar to how we had to turn the light off and on at the theater in Keysville. Charlotte's mother didn't work, but she volunteered at our school. Her dad was a salesman at a furniture store. When her dad came home, he said "Hello" to Charlotte's mother in a very monotone voice. He then walked over, sat in a big chair, and turned on the television. Charlotte ran over to him, pulling me by my hand, and introduced me. He was very polite and said very formally, as he looked at me, "Nice to meet you." He turned and continued to watch television. I did not take it personal that he didn't seem to care if he met me because I observed that this was the same way he treated Charlotte and her mother.

At Charlotte's house, everyone spoke softly to one another, unlike our home, where we were always talking and laughing rather loudly. Charlotte's mother had the dinner table set for three people. The forks, knives, and spoons were placed neatly on white cloth napkins around each plate. The napkins looked like big handkerchiefs that my dad put in his back pocket. We used paper napkins at our house. I wasn't sure what I was supposed to do with the white cloth. I watched Charlotte's parents and Charlotte put them on their laps. I followed what they did, by placing the cloth napkin on my lap, and picking the napkin up and wiping my mouth at the same time Charlotte did. After Charlotte's mother placed the dinner on the table, I bowed my head, thinking Charlotte's dad would say "Grace" as my father did before we could start eating. Charlotte and her parents looked at me, puzzled, and said, "Is anything wrong?" I lifted my head and said, "No, I'm okay." I felt really stupid. I thought everyone bowed their head and said "Grace" before eating. In our family, if we ever started eating before bowing our head, my mother would ask sternly, "Did you thank God for your food before you started eating?" It didn't matter whether we were at home or eating at McDonald's; we were still expected to bow our head and give thanks to God.

After dinner, Charlotte and I went to her room to play with her dolls. We played for quite a while before her mother told us it was time to go to bed. While Charlotte and I were talking to each other from our beds, Charlotte asked me a question that really made me feel uncomfortable. She asked, "Is that your real mother?" I answered by replying, firmly, "Yes, that's my real mother. Why did you ask me that?" She said, "Because you don't look like her. She is really pretty." I knew that Charlotte was not being mean, but I felt sad that she thought my mother wasn't my real mother, especially when she added that my mother was so pretty. Maybe she thought I was adopted because of my mother's light skin. I was always proud when Mama came to school for one of my programs, yet after Charlotte's question, I wondered if other kids thought Mama wasn't my real mother. I never told my mother what Charlotte asked me, especially since I had approached this question before. Part of me was afraid that one day Mama might tell me I was adopted. I also believed I wasn't pretty, which made me feel even more insecure. I even looked different than my sisters.

When Charlotte's mother drove me home on Saturday morning, my mother invited her in for a cup of coffee. I quickly said to Mama, "Charlotte's mother said she has to go to the grocery store." Charlotte's mother replied, "I would love to take a few moments to have coffee with your mother." I did not want Charlotte's mother to see the inside of our house, even though we always kept our house clean and neat. Actually, our house looked as well kept as Charlotte's; her house was just bigger and she had nicer furniture. Yet I thought her mother might not think we had a nice house.

During third grade, a new girl came to our class. Her name was Mary. She had long dark brown hair, which she wore in a ponytail, and dark brown eyes. Mary always wore the cutest clothes, matching sweaters with every skirt. Charlotte and I reached out to Mary since she was new in the class and she didn't know any of the other kids. The three of us were inseparable and did everything together. I was feeling happy, having two best friends, even though I didn't look like them.

Things began to change for me in fourth grade. Mary met new friends and didn't spend as much time with Charlotte and me. She still continued to be a little nicer to me than she was to Charlotte. However, sometimes she even shunned me when some of her other friends were around. Mary was turning nine and was planning a big birthday party. She asked me while we were having lunch, "Will you join me and some of the other girls to help me decide who should be invited to my party?" I felt awkward having Charlotte sitting next to me. I knew Mary was not going to include Charlotte on her birthday list; however, I could not help but feel elated that Mary included me to help decide who should come to her party. Mary said she was going to hand out the invitations the next day at school. The following day, I noticed that Mary and her new friends were a little distant toward me. Even Charlotte noticed and asked, "Is Mary mad at you?" I told Charlotte I had not done anything to make Mary mad at me. At lunch, several of the girls were giddy and excited, talking about receiving an invitation to Mary's birthday party. The school day was almost over and I still did not receive an invitation from Mary. Charlotte, who was so kind, knew that I felt bad. She said, "Why don't you just ask Mary for your invitation? I am sure she has one for you." I was afraid to ask about my invitation just in case Mary decided not to invite me. After school, I got up the courage to tell Mary that she forgot to give me an invitation. She looked very uncomfortable and embarrassed. I knew immediately that she had changed her mind and that she decided not to invite me. She looked at me with a downcast expression and said, "My mother told me that I could not invite you to my birthday party. She said that I can't be friends with you because I am getting too old to have a colored friend." I didn't understand the correlation between her turning nine and having a colored friend. For some reason, I did not have the same stinging hurt feelings that I had when the lady treated me so mean at Sears & Roebuck's. I was more angry than hurt that I was not invited to Mary's birthday party.

When I told my mother about not being invited to Mary's party she said, "Don't let one person make you feel bad. You will be invited to many other parties." I could tell by the look on Mama's face that she felt sad for me. I told myself that I didn't care about being invited to Mary's party. Charlotte would remain my best friend; however, I decided that I was going to distance myself from Mary and the other girls. I made a conscious decision that it would be better if I only had black friends; however, I didn't want to be around black kids who acted too black, by talking or laughing too loud. I didn't want white friends; I just needed to be like the white girls by emulating the things they did. I was going to have a completely new persona when I enrolled in junior high school. I would become a sophisticated black girl, who had all the trappings of being white. I told myself that things would be completely different. I was not going to allow myself to be hurt again.

Junior high school did not quite turn out the way I thought it would. It was not a positive experience for me. There was a definite division among the black and white kids. The school enrollment was made up of primarily black and white students; there were few other ethnic students who attended the school, with the exception of a few Asian students. There wasn't tension between the black and white students; each group seemed to coexist. However, there always seemed to be a conflict among black students and other blacks, especially among the girls. I was afraid to even look sideways at some of the girls or they might say, "Who you looking at?" There seemed to be a fight almost every day after school. Crowds of black kids would surround the two girls who were fighting each other. I was always frightened when these fights occurred because it didn't take much for one to become a "target." I lived one block from the school so I always ran home as quickly as possible. A girl named Norma was one of the black students whom most of the other black girls were afraid. Norma was a really big girl, not fat, but very tall. She looked more like she belonged in high school than in junior high. I really liked Norma and she liked me. We got to know each other in Art class. She would always tell me, "If anyone picks on you, I will kick their ass." That was comforting to know, but I really didn't want to be put through the test. Almost everyone was afraid of Norma; she didn't have many friends. Many of the other girls didn't get to know Norma like I did. I believe I was one of her only good friends. She had a great sense of humor, talked real loud, and laughed even more shatteringly. She was just the opposite of the "classy" black person I wanted to become. I liked Norma's genuineness and kindness that, I believe, others did not see.

Charlotte was the one white girl whom I stayed friends with. I saw to it that I included her to sit with me during lunch. My black friends didn't like having me include Charlotte when we had lunch because she was white. Regardless of how they felt, I was not going to hurt Charlotte the way I had been hurt while in grade school. Eventually, two of my friends accepted Charlotte into our group. The three of us did not live far from each other and walked home together after school. Both of my black friends were very shy and, like me, didn't want to be around girls who got into fights. One time during gym class, our gym teacher appointed me as the bathroom monitor. After he took attendance, and found out that some of the girls were missing, he assigned me to go into the bathroom and report the names of the girls who were hiding so they could skip class. When the girls found out that I had given their names to the gym teacher, they said they were all going to beat me up after school. When school got out, I ran home as quickly as I could, with a mob of kids following behind me to see the fight. I was totally out of breath when I ran inside my house. When my mother saw the mob of kids on our lawn, she said to me, "You get outside so they know you are not afraid of them." I slowly walked out onto our front porch. Mama pointed to each of them, as she roared in a very angry voice, "Which of you girls wants to fight Paula? She is right here!" My mother continued, "Her older sisters are here also. Come after her! She is not afraid of any of you!" I thought I was going to die a slow death. The entire crowd began to sluggishly walk away. My mother walked back into the house, she shook me by my shoulders and said in a very harsh tone, "I had better not ever see you let any of those girls intimidate you again or, I will spank you myself." I was really upset that my mother said this to me. It was not like my mother to speak so harshly. I dreaded going to school the next day, but knew Mama would not allow me to be a coward by staying home. I didn't ever want to fight. When the girls got in fights, they would pull each other's hair and sometimes even bite each other. The worst part was when their dresses would fly up and one could see their underwear. The kids who were watching would be laughing and egging the girls on to keep fighting. I thought it was cruel. The word got around at school that Norma was going to kick anyone's ass if they picked on me. That was the last time I got chased home.

Some of the black boys could also be rude. There was this one kid named Malcolm (pseudonym). I did not like being around him. One time when I was getting a drink of water from the water fountain, he walked up and rubbed his body against my butt. He seemed to always be taunting the girls, both black and white. He would say really gross things, suggesting that he would want to have sex with them. I was surprised that a few of the girls thought he was cute and funny. He was so crude that I didn't see anything handsome or funny about him. There was frequent gossip about Malcolm having sex with this girl or that one. I never even thought about having sex in junior high or about having a boyfriend. Although Malcolm didn't threaten any of the white boys, he still would give them mean looks when he walked by them. I was shocked when I found that both of my two best friends, whom I walked home and played with on the weekends, became pregnant by two different boys. I didn't even know who these boys were or how they met them. They were only fourteen years old. I cried along with them when they told me. Neither girl knew the other one was pregnant, until the three of us sat together at the park, where we always hung out on weekends. My parents told me I could no longer be a friend with either of the girls. I was both sad and mad at my two friends for becoming pregnant. I really cherished our friendship. Both girls dropped out of school. Although we never discussed it, I believe my friends were taken advantage of; they were both really nice girls.

I had conflicting feelings about hanging around with only black girls at school; there were some really nice white friends in some of my classes that I really liked. I began to isolate myself, not hanging around with any one person or group of kids. It did not take much for things to become volatile, just by being in the wrong place at the wrong time. I decided that I was going to go back to my original premise of being more independent. I thought this decision would keep me sheltered from all the drama of being around only black kids. I began to transform myself, by playing an instrument. This way I could be in instrumental music class with white kids. My parents bought me a used clarinet. My black friends laughed at me and said, "That's really lame! Why would you want to be in class with all those nerdy white kids?" I didn't let the comments bother me; I had already made up my mind that this was going to be the new me, not worrying about how anyone judged me. Mr. Wilson, the music teacher, had a bald head, a thick mustache, and wore thick black glasses. He yelled at

me constantly because I continued to split my clarinet reed by accidentally biting it. The other students would laugh, in a suppressed manner, when Mr. Wilson scolded me. He embarrassed me in front of the class by bellowing, "Your clarinet is not tuned. You need to take private lessons like the other students in the class so you can keep up!" I thought to myself, *If this is a beginners class, why do I need private lessons?* I thought when I enrolled in the class, Mr. Wilson would teach me how to play the clarinet...wrong! Mr. Wilson placed me in the back row of the music section. I was so humiliated, especially being the only black student in the class. There was no way my parents could afford to have me take private music lessons. I suffered through the class and received a failing grade. That was the extent of my playing the clarinet.

In History class, the students were required to do a home project, which was to be 50% of our final grade. We were to pick a city within a country and make a representation of the city in an artistic likeness of how the people may have lived. It was to be created on a big canvas, using several materials that the teacher suggested. One of the materials the teacher suggested was called Plaster of Paris. Although I had never heard of a material like this, I thought it was ironic that this was the name of the material, since I had chosen Paris as the city I wanted to present as my project. Mr. Miller, our teacher, was surprised by my choice of choosing Paris for my project. He said, "Paula, I thought you might be more interested in choosing a city from one of the countries in the continent of Africa." This made me angry, so I responded snottily, "I chose Paris because that is the city I will be visiting one day. I have no interest in doing my project from a city in one of the countries of Africa." Mr. Miller looked affronted by my arrogant response. I knew Mama would not have been happy with the way I talked to Mr. Miller, especially after she instilled in my sisters and me how to behave around whites, and particularly at school. When the project was due, my white peers brought exotic and beautiful displays of their work. I made my project using colored pencils and swizzle sticks; fortunately, we had glue at home so I was able to keep the pieces glued together. Needless to say, I received a D in this class. My project did not meet all of the teacher's criteria, even though I excelled on all the tests and participated in classroom discussions.

I continued to work hard at doing well in school in spite of not being treated very kindly by some of my teachers. I conscientiously kept under the radar by going right home after school rather than hanging around after school. I wanted to avoid any fights that might erupt. Norma and I were no longer in art class together; however, we were friendly toward one another when we saw each other in the halls. I was truly ready to move on to high school and leave the junior high school drama behind. I tried to maintain my black relationships with some of the girls, while still not wanting to be in the midst of ongoing conflicts. This was very arduous. What I longed for was to find peace in a stable environment with fewer confrontations, which I did not find while attending junior high school. I was anticipating a more positive experience at high school.

Amazing Miss Grace

My sisters and I were expected to work part-time during the school year and full-time during summer vacation. There was no lazing around at our house. In addition, we were still expected to do our assigned chores. On the weekends, we were given permission to get together with our friends at Good Park, where most of the black kids, from all over the city, hung out. There was a gigantic pool there. However, I didn't swim because I didn't want to get my hair wet. Also, when I swam, my skin became all "ashy," which meant I had to "cake" vaseline all over my body, making my skin shine like a black onyx.

Prior to attending high school, I was hired to work at Bishop Drum Nursing Home. My job at the nursing home was to pick up and clean the trays after the patients finished their meals. Cleaning dirty trays was not exactly a pleasant job; however, I made enough money to buy my own school clothes and pay for my hair to be pressed and curled. There was one patient, whose room was right next to the small kitchenette area where I cleaned the trays. Her name was Miss Gertrude. I became acquainted with her while I picked up her tray. She was so kind and seemed to enjoy my chitchatting with her. Although I knew I had vry little time to quickly pick up more trays, I never revealed to Miss Gertrude that I needed to hurry. When she sensed that I needed to leave, in her quiet voice, she said, "I really shouldn't keep you much longer. I know you have work to do." I told her I would come back when I completed my rounds and we would talk a little longer. She said, with a warm smile, "I would like that." I knew she must be lonely having to be confined to her bed. Miss

41

Gertrude wore wire-rimmed glasses, had the warmest smile, and teeth that appeared exceedingly big. Even though she was bedridden, she was amicable and gentle. She never seemed to allow her illness to affect her mood. The one thing that I never shared with anyone, because I thought it was unkind, was that something about seeing Miss Gertrude lying in her bed reminded me of the Big Bad Wolf in the children's story "Little Red Riding Hood." She was the complete antithesis of a "big bad wolf"; it was just the image of her lying in bed, with such big teeth and wire-rimmed glasses that reminded me of the childhood story.

I was pleased when Miss Gertrude's two sisters came to visit her so she would not be alone in her room. The three sisters, who were retired teachers, had all the characteristics of schoolmarms. All three knotted their hair in a bun and wore wire-rimmed glasses. The two sisters, who came to visit, wore black skirts that came down to their ankles. Both sisters were as kind and gentle-spirited as Miss Gertrude. Miss Margaret was the middle sister and Miss Grace was the youngest. Although Miss Margaret was very kind, she appeared more introverted than Miss Gertrude and Miss Grace. Miss Grace expressed to me how much she appreciated me spending time with Miss Gertrude. I told her that I enjoyed our conversations.

It seemed as though Miss Grace began to take more and more of an interest in what my future plans were. I was honest and told her that I hadn't thought much about the future, other than wanting to graduate from high school and get a good job. She smiled and said, "My two sisters and I were school teachers. We loved teaching, except we were not allowed to get married when we taught." She said with a twinkle in her eye, "Gertrude was the only one who had a serious boyfriend, but teaching was her first love." I felt somewhat uncomfortable with her sharing such personal information. I was taught that we were never to share any personal business outside of our home. However, Miss Grace was so open with me about why she and her sisters never got married; therefore, I didn't feel that I was disrespecting our family rule since I really didn't offer any personal information about my family. It seemed as though each time Miss Grace came to visit Miss Gertrude, she wanted to talk to me more about my future. I hadn't even started high school, thus, I had no idea what my future would look like. Miss Grace told me I should consider teaching as a career. She shared with me that she thought I would be an outstanding teacher based on "my patience and willingness to listen." I had never thought of myself in this way. Nevertheless, this would not be an option for me; I knew that I would not be attending college. However, I did remember how much I loved "playing" school with my friends when I was younger. I always wanted to be the teacher in front of the classroom. Miss Grace's comments ignited in me a desire to begin visualizing myself as a teacher. I continued to take time to talk to Miss Gertrude and her sisters for the remainder of the summer, especially Miss Grace. Admittedly, my focus on attending high school was much more important to me at this time. Still, I was going to miss seeing the sisters when school started in the fall. I was somewhat sad when I said goodbye to the three sisters, believing I may not see them again. We had not shared contact information. Besides, I wasn't sure that there would be any point in our continuing to talk. I inquired if there was part-time work that I could do after school; unfortunately, my supervisor told me there were no openings. I was disappointed, though not surprised since this was a small nursing home. I began to look for other part-time work and applied to several places where it would be convenient for me to take public transportation. I was surprised and elated when I received a call from Bishop Drum Nursing Home, just a week before high school started, inquiring if I would like to work three days a week after school and every other weekend. I was looking forward to making money, but I really appreciated that I would be able to continue conversing with the three sisters. This was the first personal and genuine friendship I had formed with white adults. I didn't realize at the time what an amazing influence Grace would have on my future. It placed me on a trajectory that would shape my future. I will be forever grateful and blessed that God placed Miss Grace in my life.

Miss Betty June's Beauty Shop

I continued to emulate my white peers. I took tap dancing lessons at the Jewish Community Center, for free, and swung my long ponytail back and forth. In order to keep my ponytail swinging and my hair straight, my mother took me, twice a month, to Miss Betty June's Beauty Shop. I loved getting my hair pressed, and liked how shiny and much longer my hair looked after it was straightened with a hot comb. In addition to attending Union Baptist Church, going to Miss Betty June's Shop kept me feeling connected to my black roots. Going to Miss Betty June's Beauty Shop was an all-day event. Mama dropped me off at 8:00 in the morning and picked me up around 5:00 in the evening, or whenever Miss Betty June would call her and tell her I was ready. Many daughters came with their mothers to get their hair styled; Mama didn't get her hair styled at the black beauty shop because she had what black people called "white people's hair." She did her own hair at home; seldom did she go to a white beauty salon unless she needed her hair to be colored, or to get a haircut.

Most black women are fixated on their hair, including me. Keeping our hair "done," as we say, makes us feel good. My mother's friend used to say, "Even if I don't have a decent pair of shoes on, my hair is going to be done!" Black hair will frizz if it gets wet, which is why most black women detest having their hair get wet. Getting caught in the rain, without an umbrella, may be a black woman's worse nightmare. A black woman regards her hair "being done" as the finishing touch to complement her attire. A priority for most women of color, during that time, was to make sure she had made an appointment to get her hair styled for Saturday morning. Some of the clients at Miss Betty June's had "standing" appointments so they didn't have to worry about not being able to get in. On Saturdays, the beauty shop was busy the entire day. Miss Betty June orchestrated everything and everyone in her shop. When clients came in, she directed them to which beautician they would be seeing. She had her own "regulars" that only came to her. She was rather bossy, but also very kind at the same time. She was exquisitely dressed, wearing big earrings, clunky jewelry, high-heeled shoes (which she took off when her feet got tired), fake long eyelashes, and wore make-up galore. She slicked her hair back in a French roll, which made her look very exotic. All the hairdressers laughed clamorously and gossiped in somewhat hushed voices about the other women in town. If the kids seemed to be listening, one of the hairdressers would say to them, "Quit being so nosey and go outside and play until we call you in to get your hair done." The women were seated in chairs lined up against the wall waiting to be called "next" by one of the hairdressers. The hairdressers would start on one client's hair by putting on color or relaxer and then have that client seated while the hairdresser called another client to her chair. There didn't seem to be an organized system as to who would be next. However, the clients didn't mind waiting. For these women, it was a day off from work, having time to relax, and to socialize with their kindred "sisters." It was a time for them to feel carefree and happy. Having their hair done seemed secondary to why they came to the beauty shop.

All the clients and the beauty operators were excited when the church-women arrived with fried chicken, catfish, collard greens, mashed potatoes, macaroni and cheese, and hot buttered cornbread. Mama always gave me a few dollars so I could buy a couple of the delicious fried chicken wings and a piece of warm buttery cornbread. When the food arrived, all hair production stopped while the hairdressers and clients took their break to eat. The high-spirited laughter and talking continued throughout the eating ceremony. When the first round of food was gone, the churchwomen would return to the church and bring another round of food to the beauty shop. The hair-dressers were always nice about making sure the kids got their food first. After Miss Betty June thought enough time had been spent on socializing and eating, she would announce, "Okay, y'all, if we are going to get outta here by 5:00 (which they never did), then it's time to get back to work!" The hairdressers would scurry back to their chairs and resume working on their clients.

Although I knew I would be spending long hours on Saturdays at the beauty shop, Miss Betty June's Beauty Shop was memorable, an experience I will always remember. I continue this tradition. Taunya, my hair stylist, knows I will be arriving at 8 A.M. sharp every Saturday morning. Today, however, the clients are much more subdued and sophisticated. The "shops" have become "beauty salons," and there are no more church ladies delivering fried chicken and catfish. I observe women, looking at their watches, anxiously waiting for the hairstylist (no longer called hairdresser) to start on their hair. Most women sit quietly, looking or texting on their iPhones, maybe giving a quick nod to another client, but clearly not eager to start up a conversation. I realize that this part of my culture will never be rekindled.

The Balancing Act

High school was a welcome relief from junior high school. I spent all three years of high school riding the bus with Arthurlene, one of my best friends. Arthurlene lived not too far from my neighborhood. Arthurlene seemed so mature, confident, and serious. She also was very intelligent. I felt a little intimidated around her, feeling less mature and not as smart. If anyone should be attending college, it definitely should have been Arthurlene. The two of us bonded really well and had fun together. We used to smoke cigarettes together on our way to school. If my parents had ever found out, I would be on punishment for weeks! Besides, I knew my parents would be very disappointed in me since I was pretty compliant and seldom caused them any problems. Actually, we were pretty nice girls, maybe even on the nerdy side; smoking cigarettes gave us that little edge of being "cool." We were together before school, during lunch, and rode home on the bus together after school.

The majority of the students who attended North High were white and the only minority on staff were Mr. Spriggs, a math teacher, and Miss Johnson, the attendance clerk. All the other staff and faculty were white. Many of the black kids hung out in the front hall near the entrance of the school. I disliked walking by the boys because they made remarks like, "Look at you, girl! What you doing later?" I was already shy, which no one knew or believed; I did a good job of faking it. However, it was difficult for me to pass by the boys every day. If I didn't smile or say "Hi," they would say, "So you think you too good to speak?"

The school seemed so big when I first started. I had problems figuring out where my classes were the first day of school. I was afraid that I would be late and get scolded by my teachers in front of the class. I was happy when a senior student, named Donna, came up to me and asked if I needed help. She told me that she was a Senior Ambassador and was assigned to new students who may need help with their schedules or finding classes. I didn't know that students could be Ambassadors; I had only learned later, in History class, about the role of Ambassadors and how they were goodwill representatives for the United States and were placed in other countries. Donna was very kind; she even walked me to my first class, which was English. When I entered the classroom, Mr. Wickman smiled at me and told me to take any seat. I hesitated, not knowing where I should sit. I didn't recognize anyone; however, what I did notice was that I was the only black student in the class. Mr. Wickman made me feel very comfortable, which was why English became my favorite class. Mr. Wickman was a great teacher and made learning interesting and fun. The research I conducted for my doctoral dissertation: *Black Students' Voices: Experiences and Perspectives Around Attending an Affluent Majority White Suburban High School*, asserted that black students perform, academically stronger, if they have a positive relationship with their teachers. The research noted, white students were more likely to be concerned about their grades, regardless of their relationship with their teachers.

I enjoyed most of my other classes and became casual friends with some of the white kids in my classes; however, we seldom socialized outside of school. Blacks and whites during the 1960s still socialized within their own ethnic groups, after school and on weekends. There was one class I despised; that was my History class. I hated Black History Month. My history teacher, Mr. Troe, would continually ask my opinion about my views on the Civil Rights Movement or how I felt about Martin Luther King or Malcolm X, as though I was the classroom expert regarding these topics. I felt extremely humiliated and embarrassed when he called on me. I wanted to feign illness and run out of the room. It felt as if all the other students turned around and stared at me, waiting for me to answer the questions.

During my sophomore year, one of my white friends, Pam, asked me to try out for cheerleading with her. I did not let any of my black friends know, afraid they may laugh or make some negative remarks. However, I decided to try out and was extremely nervous during the audition. I left quickly afterwards, not even talking to Pam. Luckily, since I had missed the first bus, I took the later bus so was spared having to see Jesserean or Arthurlene. The cheerleading coach told the girls that she would post the names on the bulletin board, listing the names of the girls who made the cheerleading squad. The next day I was afraid to see if my name was on the list so I asked Pam to look for me. She came back and sadly reported, "Your name was not on the list." Pam made the cheerleading squad, which I could tell made her feel sad for me. I was angry for allowing myself to audition. I knew, during the audition, that I was not as good as the other girls and certainly not as confident. I was proud of myself for at least trying out. I found out later that several of the girls, who tried out, had attended a cheerleaders' camp during the summer. I wasn't aware that there were cheerleading camps. The only camp that I had ever attended was the Salvation Army Camp when I was younger. Many of my black friends also attended the same camp. Daily, we sang the "Salvation Army Camp" song. I, vividly, still remember all the words of the song today.

High school was a lot mellower than junior high. Most of the students were pleasant and there was not a lot of drama that I experienced while in junior high school. My parents were a lot less strict and permitted me to go to dances at the Wilkie House, which was a community center where black kids hung out on weekends. My father would drop me off and pick me up at exactly 11:00 P.M. A lot of the kids would remain outside rather than inside where the dancing was. I was forbidden to ever be outside. Daddy made it clear by saying, "If I drive by and see you hanging around outside, that's the last time you go, and you can kiss the Wilkie House goodbye." Sometimes my friends would tell me that they saw my father drive by. I knew he was checking to see if I was outside; he feared that I could be in harm's way by being outside. Admittedly, arguments and fights generally did start outside. In fact, there actually were guys who "packed" guns, and threatened to use them. Unlike in junior high where girls were the ones who were the fighters; the boys were the ones who got into "territorial" arguments and ended up fighting. The fights usually happened between the Southside boys and the Westside boys. The Westside guys did not like the Southside guys flirting with the girls from the Westside. The Southside boys had a bad reputation for coming from the "wrong side" of the tracks much similar to the movie *Westside Story*. My father exclaimed, "Nothing good happens outside the Wilkie House, that's why you need to stay inside." Besides the fights that occurred, a lot of "making out" took place in the cars that were parked outside. I was tempted a few times to sit in the car with one of the boys I liked, but knew I would suffer the consequences if my father ever caught me. Especially since I wasn't supposed to have a boyfriend in the first place.

Almost every Monday morning, before school, the black kids stood in the front hall and talked about Saturday night at the Wilkie House. I overheard guys talking about a girl he "got over with." We girls spent time talking about this guy who always tried to kiss us with wet slimy lips. We also talked about hating to slow dance with this other guy because he always pulled us too close and tried to wrap his leg around one of our legs. When we saw him walk toward one of us, we would quickly pretend we were on our way to the restroom. Monday morning gossip sessions made me uncomfortable, not knowing if I would become the next hot topic of discussion. As soon as the warning bell rang, we all scurried to our classes before the final ring blasted. Unlike junior high, black friends hung around after school, talking and making plans for the weekend. I did not notice white kids hanging out in a big group before or after school. I attribute the need for black kids to congregate together as a way of "belonging." There were only two high schools where the majority of black students attended, one on the east side of town and the other on the north side of town. Because of the small population of blacks in Des Moines, many of us knew students from the other schools.

College recruiters came to school during my junior year of high school. They were from colleges all over the United States. An announcement came over the intercom during homeroom, stating the college recruiters would be available to talk to juniors and seniors during lunch period. Lunch period was extended so students would have an opportunity to meet with the recruiters. Many of my white friends were bubbling with excitement, going from table to table anxious to speak to different college recruiters. The recruiters were lined up behind tables outside the lunchroom. The students who weren't interested in speaking with the college recruiters were happy to have the extended lunch period to hang out with friends. Several friends asked me which of the recruiters I was interested in speaking with. I hadn't planned on speaking to any of them. I believed college was not an option for me. I had considered attending a business school as a possible option. Not wanting my white friends to know that I wasn't going to college, I told them that I was going to walk around each table to assess if any of the college materials looked interesting.

One of the recruiters stopped me just as I was picking up a brochure, pretending I was interested. He had a warm smile and a gentle demeanor. He asked me, as I flipped through the brochure, "Have you ever heard of Yankton College in South Dakota?" I began thinking to myself, *I don't even know exactly where South Dakota is located, much less anything about the college.* I began stammering and said, "No, sir, I have never heard about that college." He said, "Would you like to hear about the school?" Not wanting to be rude, I replied, "yes sir. I would be interested in learning about the college." He continued to tell me that Yankton was a small college located on a beautiful campus. He picked up a brochure and pointed to a picture of the campus. He told me about the different majors that were offered. He asked me had I thought about my major. My conversation with Grace came to my mind, remembering that she told me that I would be a good teacher. I quickly lied by saying, "I am going to major in education and become a teacher." "That's great!" he said. He proceeded to tell me about Yankton having an outstanding education program. I was becoming so anxious and wanted this whole conversation to end so I could escape. I did not want to speak with another recruiter. However, I was polite and continued to listen to his spiel. He said, "Why don't you look over the materials with your parents and consider sending in an application?" I told him I would do so, just wanting badly to end any further discussion about the college. He requested that I write down my name, address, and phone number and said that he would follow up with me. He was serious! Did he really want me to consider Yankton College? Besides knowing that I would not be able to attend, I thought the college sounded like a hokey school located in a faraway place.

The following day, my white friends continued to be excited about meeting with the college recruiters, discussing the colleges they were thinking about applying to. Several asked me what college I was most interested in. I just shrugged and said I didn't know. I was too embarrassed to tell them that I had only spoken to one recruiter, and only because he approached me. Still, there was a certain exhilaration I felt about the possibility of going to college. I told a few of my black friends about talking to the recruiter about Yankton College in South Dakota. They laughed hilariously and said, "You can't be serious! There are no black people in South Dakota." One of the friends said, "Why did you give that man your number? What if he really calls you? You know you ain't going to that college!" I was so humiliated, while feeling angry at the same time. I felt dumb for even talking to the recruiter, yet I was disgusted with my black friends for not even looking at any of the college materials. I decided not to mention anything to my parents about my discussion with the college recruiter.

I was pleased that I had to work after school. I would be busy at work and didn't have to think about the college recruiter or about my friends making fun of me. I looked forward to seeing Miss Gertrude and hoped her two sisters were coming to visit. When I delivered Miss Gertrude's tray, both sisters were sitting in the room. For some reason I had a nervous feeling. I had an urge to tell Miss Grace about talking to the college recruiter, but then thought it was better if I didn't. After I picked up all the trays, I took my time wiping off the plates and putting them in the dishwasher, hoping the two sisters might be gone by the time I finished. I decided I didn't want to talk to Miss Grace tonight about the recruiter, but I still wanted to say goodnight to Miss Gertrude before I left. Just as I was going to check to see if the two sisters had left, Miss Grace poked her head in the kitchenette door and inquired, "How are you today?" I could tell that Miss Grace sensed something might be wrong. She continued by saying, "You don't seem your perky little self." I responded, "I am fine. I just have things on my mind." Miss Grace looked concerned and said, "Can I help with anything?" I took a deep breath and shared with her the conversation I had with the college recruiter. I begin speaking to her, almost inaudibly, about how the college recruiter requested that I fill out an application and how I lied to him by telling him I wanted to be a teacher. I also told Miss Grace that the recruiter was going to follow up by calling me. I told her how foolish it was for me to give him my phone number. I did not want him to call my home because my parents would be very upset that I gave my number to a stranger. I continued to babble on and on, until I burst into tears. Miss Grace looked at me as though she was trying to understand all that I was telling her; she was confused about why I was so upset. She said to me, "Why are you so upset about the college recruiter wanting you to fill out a college application?" She continued, "That does not mean you have to go to that college. There are plenty of other colleges you may consider." I pulled myself together and explained to her it was not about attending Yankton College that upset me. I told her it was because I knew it was not possible for me to attend college. She said, "So if it were possible, you would want to attend college?" I looked up at her and said, "After talking to the recruiter today. I started feeling I really would like to go to college." Surprisingly, Miss Grace, who generally was seldom animated, looked at me with the warmest smile. For some reason she looked much taller than I had envisioned her to be before. She had her arms folded and stood so straight, almost statuesque. She said, "Paula, that's wonderful news!" I had never heard her say my name so emphatically. She shared with me that she was familiar with Yankton College and believed it would be a perfect school for me. She asked, "Why don't you bring the application to work tomorrow and we will go over it together?" Miss Grace offered to speak to my mother about what a great opportunity going to college would be for me. I was not keen on Miss Grace talking to my mother; I had not told my parents about the college recruiter or the college, but thought it might be easier if Miss Grace talked to my mother. Miss Grace called my mother that same evening. Mama was a little confused by the call, but was very gracious and told Miss Grace how much she appreciated her kindness and that she would have to give more thought about me applying for a college in another state. Mama was a little upset with me for not telling her about my talking to the recruiter and especially for not forewarning her that Miss Grace was going to call her. My mother talked to my father. His response was, "That's the craziest thing I ever heard of." He stated adamantly, "Paula needs to stay right here in Des Moines, Iowa, and get a good job at the telephone company." Working at the telephone company was a prestigious place to work, especially for black female graduates who graduated with good grades. Ironically, I was given similar advice from several of my teachers at North High School. My journalism teacher, Mr. Barnett, was the only teacher who talked to me about attending college. Expectations were low for black students; many teachers did not believe that black students were "college material."

Miss Grace, who continued to be my lifeline, assisted me with filling out the college application. I hesitantly mailed in the application and requested that the high school send in my transcripts. In two months I received a personal call from Mr. Green, the college recruiter. My sister, Dorothy Ann, yelled to me and said, "Paula, there's some white man on the phone from Yankton College who wants to talk to you!" I ran to the phone, happy that neither Mama nor Daddy was at home. I was so nervous when I picked up the phone. Mr. Green introduced himself on the phone, reminding me of talking to me at school. He said he wanted to call me personally. I hardly heard the words, "Congratulations, you have been accepted to Yankton College!" I was both ecstatic yet frightened at the same time. I was actually speechless. Mr. Green explained to me that I would be receiving a formal letter of acceptance and would be invited to attend college Spring Break Weekend my senior year of high school. My heart began to flutter as reality set in. I don't even remember if I thanked him before we hung up. All I could think about was, *Why did I get my hopes up? I am not going to be able to go to Yankton College or any college for that matter.* I knew my parents could not afford for me to go to college, and, I certainly did not make enough money at Bishop Drum Nursing Home. I didn't talk to my parents about the call I received from Mr. Green or the college acceptance letter I would be receiving in the mail. I knew my mother would feel sad for me and my father would say it was idiotic that I would even consider such an outlandish thought. I had to decide what I was going to do with the acceptance letter, since it required that my parents sign it, indicating that they approved of my attending the college, as well as other commitments involved attending the college. During that time, parents were completely involved in decisions about college, including directly receiving student grades.

The next day at work I was feeling very dejected, not wanting to see Gertrude or the two sisters. I didn't want to continue with the whole college discussion. I knew if I saw Miss Grace it would be inevitable that the topic would come up. When I went in Miss Gertrude's room to pick up her tray, I pretended to be in a big hurry and apologized that I didn't have time to chat. Both sisters were in the room and I politely greeted them as I rushed out of the room. I was shocked when Miss Grace came into the kitchenette. She had never walked directly into the kitchenette before. She quietly said to me, "Do you have a moment to talk to me when you are done with work?" I wanted to say "no," but did not want to be disrespectful by denying her request. I said, quietly, "Yes, of course, I have time to speak with you." After work, Miss Grace said that she had requested a private room for the two of us to speak. I was visibly shaking. Why did she want a private room for us to speak? She appeared so serious. Miss Grace started the conversation by asking if I had heard back from the college. I began to cry, not whimpering, but sobbing loudly with tears streaming down my face. I looked up at Miss Grace and saw her kind and apologetic expression. She cradled me in her long arms and said, "I am so sorry you were not accepted. There is still the junior college where you can get started." I tried vehemently to stop crying and to get my breath. With a forced smile I said, "Miss Grace, Mr. Green called me and told me that I have been accepted." Then I proceeded to start crying all over again. Miss Grace took her arms down from my shoulders and looked at me with confusion. She grabbed both of my hands and said, "That's wonderful! Are you sad because you don't want to go?" I explained to her, "I do want to go, but I know I can't go because my parents can't afford it, and my father doesn't want me to go anyway." She looked me straight in my eyes and said, "You must go! It is very important that a smart Negro girl like you go to college." She had never alluded to me as being Negro. I wasn't sure how to take this remark. Should I be offended? I told her I would talk to my mother when I got home; still feeling very uncomfortable with her last remark. I for sure was not going to talk to my father about any plans about going to college. I spoke to my mother about receiving a call from the college, informing me that I had been accepted. I quickly assured Mama that I had no expectations of attending, knowing there was no way we could afford for me to go. I proceeded to tell Mama about what Miss Grace said to me. I thought my mother would be shocked hearing about Miss Grace referring to me as a Negro. My mother looked at me warmly and said, "Miss Grace didn't say that to offend you. She really cares about you and feels it is important for you to go to college so you can succeed in life." She went on to say, "Miss Grace really believes in you and that's very special." My mother had a wonderful way in believing that most people had sincere intentions, especially good-hearted people like Miss Grace. That night, as I was lying in bed, I began to think of myself as a college student.

A Dream Fulfilled

Miss Grace shared with me that she contacted Yankton College, unbeknown to me, to inquire about scholarship opportunities. She told me that she also wanted me to do "my part" in investigating the availability of other scholarships. I believe she was helping me become more self-directed in learning how to advocate for myself. It wasn't that I wanted her to do everything for me; it was just that I had never had anyone mentor to me the same way she did in regard to preparing for college. Miss Grace said to me, "Your college counselor will also help you find resources that provide opportunities to apply for scholarships." My response was, "To be honest, I don't think I have a college counselor." I really felt stupid not knowing that I should have been talking to a college counselor. I found out from my white friends that they had met with their college counselor on several occasions. The students told me that the college counselor had set up appointments with them at the beginning of the year to go over their transcripts, to help with college applications, and to keep track of deadlines for applying for scholarships. I approached Jesserean and Arthurlene, "Did your counselor contact you to talk about college scholarships?" Although I did not remember either Jesserean or Arthurlene talking about plans to attend college; Jesserean, who was one to give you that irritated look, by rolling her eyes and laughing sardonically, reacted with impatience, "What a ridiculous question! What made you ask us that? Of course we have not been contacted any more than you have." It made me angry to think that the counselors appeared to have very little interest in encouraging black students to attend college, much less talk to them about available scholarships.

Miss Grace had become my college counselor. I solicited Miss Grace's help in looking over several scholarships that were being offered in *Ebony Magazine*, a magazine that was targeted for blacks. It was the "go-to" celebrity gossip magazine, as well as included inspirational articles, fashion, and helpful information about careers. *Ebony Magazine* published that more than 1000 scholarships, annually, went unapplied by black students. Many black students, just as I, believed that college was unattainable. I was inspired and encouraged by Miss Grace to pursue college scholarships on my own. I saw two scholarships, in *Ebony Magazine*, being offered to students who were majoring in education. I applied and received $500 from one business organization, and $1000 from another. Each required typewritten essays on why I wanted to become a teacher. My typing teacher gave me permission to stay after school to use one of the typewriters, since I did not have one at home. Miss Grace also read over my essays and helped me with grammar and sentence structure, wanting to help me send in compelling essays. I was so proud of myself for submitting the applications and receiving the scholarships. Two months after, I sent in my scholarship application to Yankton College. Several weeks later, a letter arrived in the mail with the Yankton College insignia on the envelope. I was so excited that I took the envelope to my room, where I could open it alone, afraid to know what was in the contents. I tore open the envelope and had to read the letter twice. The letter stated that I had received a full-tuition scholarship to attend Yankton College! I ran done the steps, screaming while jumping up and down. "I got it, I got it, I got it!" My mother ran out of the kitchen holding her chest inquiring, "What on earth is wrong?" My sisters were yelling, "Paula's gone crazy!" I could hardly get the words out to tell them about my good news. When everyone understood what I was saying, they all yelled along with me, while jumping up and hugging me at the same time. I could hardly wait for Daddy to come home to give him the good news. I kept running to the window each time I thought I heard his car drive into the driveway. When he finally drove up, I ran to the car and opened his car door before he could even turn the car off, while happily jumping up and down. "What's going on, Puddin' (nickname he called me)? What's so important that you can't wait until I can at least get out of the car?" I enthusiastically said, "I got a big scholarship from Yankton College!" My father, who always worked at keeping his feelings "close to his chest," said somewhat irritated, "Let me at least get in the house so you can tell me what you are talking about." I was a little deflated that this was my father's response, but also knew this was his way of being overly cautious, until he understood the full scope of what I was trying to convey to him. Once he walked in the house, with me walking swiftly behind, he walked over and kissed my mother, which he did every evening when Mama greeted him at the door. "I am going to go upstairs, wash up, and take off my uniform." My feelings were hurt. Daddy did not ask me one word about what I wanted to say to him. When he came downstairs, he looked at me, "Now tell me about this good news you are so excited about." I said to him less excited, "I was trying to tell you about the scholarship I received from Yankton College." Daddy looked at me and commented, "I still don't understand why you need to go to a college so far away, in no-man's land. But that is good news." In spite of his flat response, I knew Daddy well enough to know he was proud. This was Daddy's way of telling me that he didn't want me to leave home. He asked me a lot of questions about the college and continued to inquire about why I didn't just attend the junior college in town. Later that evening, I realized that if it weren't for the fact that I stopped to talk to the college recruiter, I wouldn't have given attending college much thought. Miss Grace's belief in me also began to influence my thinking about the possibility of attending college. I thought more about Miss Grace and what a wonderful mentor she was to me.

College Orientation Weekend

After much discussion and convincing my father of how much I wanted to attend college weekend, my parents agreed that I could attend College Orientation Weekend in the spring of my senior year. I had butterflies just thinking about what it would be like visiting Yankton College for the first time. I continued to imagine how I would feel walking around campus and living in a dormitory. Drake University's campus was the only college campus I had been on, with my sisters and friends, when we attended the annual Drake Relays. I had never thought of Drake University as a place I would attend college. My only other association with Drake was when I was dating a really nice student, who attended the university when he was a freshman while I was a senior in high school.

My mother cried when she put me on the bus, by myself, to travel to South Dakota, a place that seemed so remote and foreign to me. The excitement of going away to college overcame my fear of riding on the bus alone. Daddy gave me $20 before he left for work along with a litany of rules: "Don't talk to any strangers. Keep your head straight ahead and make no contact with anyone! When the bus makes stopovers, get off the bus only to go to the restroom and return immediately back on the bus! Sit up front by the driver." Mama gave me four quarters to keep in a small coin bag. I was instructed to save the quarters for emergencies in case I had to call home "collect" from a phone booth.

It seemed as though the bus made a trillion stops along the way. I thought we would never get to the campus. I was relieved when we finally arrived. The bus station was this tiny little blue building that looked like a little house. It seemed to be in the middle of nowhere. Until I saw Mr. Green's smiling face, I felt a tinge of nervousness, wondering what I had gotten myself into. Mr. Green, the recruiter, whom I had communications with about the college at my high school, came up and warmly greeted me warmly, as well as the other visiting students, who were on the same bus. The other students had flown in from various cities across the country and had taken the bus from Sioux City, Iowa, to Yankton. I was not aware that we were all coming to the same place until we arrived at Yankton. None of us acknowledged the other during the bus ride. I was intent on keeping my head straight, focusing on what to expect during the college visit. Mr. Green gathered us all together and had us introduce ourselves. Realization hit me that I was the only black student. I didn't feel that anyone looked at me strange; however, I began to feel out of place. As I began to notice that the other students seemed just as nervous about being on campus and seeing students they had never met; I relaxed and tried not to focus on my insecurity of being the only black person in the group. One thing that stood out to me was how elegantly casual the other students were dressed. To me, they all reeked of money; the girls wearing crisp white blouses, pleated plaid skirts, and penny-loafer shoes; the guys wearing pressed khaki pants. They also were wearing penny-loafers. I was overdressed, wearing a fancy dress and black pumps, finding quickly this was not "campus" attire. When I returned home I bought a September edition of *Seventeen* magazine, which featured the "in" look for college students to wear.

Mr. Green asked each of us to tell why we had chosen Yankton, I froze. No way was I going to say because it was the only college table I stopped at when the recruiters came to my high school. I mumbled something incoherent like, "I heard it was a really good college." Mr. Green assured us that we were going to enjoy the weekend. He gave each of us a packet of information. The other girls and I warmed up quickly to each other, asking such questions about where we were from and how we knew about the college. The boys were a little more standoffish. They didn't even talk to each other. I was awestruck when we drove to campus. It was a beautiful setting with rolling green hills. It was breathtakingly beautiful. The air had a distinctive fresh smell, and the buildings were old, but quaint and strikingly elegant.

All of the students were brought into the common courtyard and were given a map of the campus and the name of the person who we would be rooming with for the weekend. One of our activities was to walk around and introduce ourselves, tell where we were from, and to see if the person's name on their nametag had the same room number as the one on our nametag. I was so excited when I met the person I would be rooming with. Betsy (pseudonym) was from New Jersey. She had a really unusual, but cute, accent and a head full of curly blonde hair. I had never been to New Jersey so was unaware that people from the East Coast spoke differently than the people from Iowa. Actually, the only other cities I had visited were Nebraska, California, and Missouri. My Aunt Frances and Aunt Lillie Ann had a little bit of a southern accent, but Betsy's accent seemed really different. New Jersey sounded exotic. Betsy told me she lived near the "shore." I wasn't sure what it would be like to live by a "shore," but it sounded glamorous.

Betsy and I became friends immediately and hung out together the entire weekend. We both loved the campus tour and were exceptionally excited about visiting the dormitory and seeing the rooms where we would be staying. When it was time to leave, we exchanged addresses and promised to write each other over the summer. Both of us expressed how happy we were that we would be roommates when we returned to college in the fall. Betsy and I continued to stay in contact, by writing letters to each other. We even talked about what each of us should bring to our dorm room. She said she could bring a record player and I said I would bring an alarm clock, one for each of us. Betsy and I spent our free time walking around campus, laughing and talking with some of the other girls we met. I enjoyed eating in the cafeteria with them. Like me, I could tell all the girls were a little uncomfortable, meeting other new girls for the first time. They, nervously but animated, were trying hard to be natural and keep conversations going. A couple of the girls said they were having their cars shipped to school. Others said their parents were driving their cars to school and were flying back home. A few of the girls stood smiling, but not saying too much. I fit into that group. I was guarded, not wanting to share too much about me. I felt out of my league. Daddy used to say when he was around rich people, "You could smell the green stuff," meaning the people had a lot of money. I could "smell the green stuff," dripping from these girls. However, they were very nice and caused me to not think about being the only black.

All I could think about while riding back home on the Greyhound Bus, was what it was going to be like being a college student at Yankton College. I even surprised myself about not feeling nervous about going so far away from home. I believe I was ready for a change. I felt that I had outgrown Des Moines.

The Senior Banquet

During my last year of high school my mind was consumed with what it would be like to start college next year. Even though I had received a scholarship, which would cover tuition, I had trepidations regarding how I was going to pay for my books and other expenses. My friends were in disbelief that I was considering going away to college in South Dakota. I had made up my mind that I wasn't going to worry about the "how" and just relish in believing that everything was going to work out. On the door of the counselor's office was a long list of seniors' names, listing the students who had been accepted to different colleges. My name was not on the list. When I asked the College Counselor's Secretary why my name had been omitted, she said no one told her that I had been accepted to a college. She had that surprised look on her face as if to say, "I am surprised that you are going to college." My feelings were hurt, but I was proud of myself by saying kindly, "Tomorrow I will bring you my acceptance letter." I had already given a copy to my counselor, but she obviously didn't look at it or didn't take it too seriously.

I usually looked forward to summers, not having homework or having to get up for school, and just relax after work. However, when I returned back from College Weekend, all I could think about was graduating from high school and beginning college in the fall. I still did not have enough money to pay all of my college expenses. Miss Grace offered to pay for my books and Mr. Green, the college recruiter, told me that there would be campus jobs available. Knowing this relieved some of the stress I was feeling about covering all my expenses. Mama told me that she would try to send additional spending money, when she had it, to pay for other incidentals that I would need. My father began to warm up to the idea of my going away to college. I eavesdropped and heard him bragging to his Friday night buddies, saying, "My Paula will be leaving for college soon." His friends replied by giving him a "high-five" and saying, "George, that's wonderful. You must be proud as a rooster." Daddy said, "Yeah, I am. Just wish she wasn't going away so far." They all nodded their heads, looking somewhat melancholy, as they continued to pass around their usual pint of Jim Beam whiskey in the brown paper bag.

I continued to study hard so I could maintain a 3.5 grade point average for the remainder of my senior year. Some of the seniors stopped taking the last semester of high school very seriously, but I didn't want to do anything that would jeopardize my future plans. I wanted all my focus to be on graduating and preparing for college.

One of the administrators, Miss Lyons, who was the Girls' Advisor and Senior Class Sponsor, seemed to take a liking to me, perhaps because I worked as an office assistant where she saw me often.

Miss Lyon's Girl's Advisor

She frequently walked down the hall very fast, as though she was on her way to an urgent meeting. Her glasses were propped on top of her head and she usually wore a cardigan sweater, red plaid pleated long skirt, with a white-laced handkerchief partially tucked in her waistband. Whenever she saw me in the hall, she generally would stop, very rushed, and say, "Keep up the good work," and continue on her way. I never felt her comments were compliments because she wasn't as kind to the other black students. They told me how she would rush by them and never say a word, much less look at them. I believed what Miss Lyons was really saying, "You are different because you are not like the other black students."

One day while I was working in the front office, Miss Lyons requested that I come to her office. She said she would like to speak to me privately. Usually when girls were called into Miss Lyons' office, it was because they had done something wrong. I was surprised when Miss Lyons told me she wanted to talk to me because she selected me to be on the Senior Banquet Planning Committee. I was honored because this committee was thought of as a very prestigious committee. Miss Lyons personally selected the seniors, with whom she referred to as the "cream of the crop," to serve on the Senior Banquet Committee. I had never seen a black student serve on the Senior Banquet Committee so felt honored that I was selected. The primary responsibilities of this committee were to select every detail of the event, which included selecting a theme, selecting a community guest speaker, selecting a male and female speaker, and arranging all the seat assignments. Since I was on the sub-committee in charge of working with another senior in assigning seats, I took this as an opportunity to place Jesserean and Arthurlene at my table. When the committee sat down to ensure that all the details had been completed, Miss Lyons looked closely at the seating arrangements. I was hoping she wouldn't notice that I placed my friends at my table. She looked at the seating arrangement again and then narrowed her eyes as she looked up at me. She became furious and said to me, "There will be no table with three black students sitting together." She continued, "I am disappointed that you would try to get away with trying to manipulate the seating for your selfish purpose!" The other committee members looked down, extremely uncomfortable. Miss Lyons told me that I would need to rearrange the seats so my black friends would be dispersed among the white students. I shocked myself by the way I responded back to Miss Lyon, not obeying the family "mantra" regarding how we were to speak to white people, and to not do anything that would cause me to get into trouble at school. I said to Miss Lyons in a firm and forceful voice, "I have every right to sit with my friends just as the white kids can sit at a table with all white students." The way Miss Lyons looked at me, I could tell she was surprised by the way I spoke to her. She responded by saying to me, "You are being disrespectful and not obeying me; therefore, you will not be coming to the Senior Banquet." This was the first time I found my "voice" by saying, "We will see about that!" I stomped out of her office and left school, with tears streaming down my face. I was dreading facing Mama's reaction when the school called to report that I left school and how I had talked to Miss Lyons. I was even more afraid of how angry Daddy was going to be when he got home. My mother was waiting at the door when I walked in. She said to me, "Let's sit down. I want to know, from you, exactly what happened in Miss Lyons' office today." I was sobbing so hard that I could hardly talk. I finally got up the courage to tell Mama what I said to Miss Lyons and why I got so mad at her. My mother sat straight up in her chair and looked at me with a long stare. I wasn't sure what was going to happen next. I was waiting for her to admonish me, yet I was still so angry with Miss Lyons that I was prepared for any discipline coming to me. My mother stood up and said quietly but forceful, "Tomorrow morning, I am coming to school with you to see Miss Lyons." She continued, "You and your friends will be sitting at the same table!" She told me to go upstairs and change my clothes, she added, "You are never to leave school again, without my permission." My head was in a fog. I wasn't sure what Mama was going to say to Miss Lyons. I figured that I definitely had been removed from the committee.

My mother never took off from work, unless one of the kids was sick and even then she often had one of the older sisters stay home from school to babysit. Mama and I took the bus together, not really talking to each other. My mother looked in deep thought so I opened my Spanish book, pretending I was studying. When we arrived at school, my mother instructed me to go to my class. I thought she wanted me to go with her to Miss Lyons' office, but she looked at me, with her expressive eyes and said, "I want to speak to Miss Lyons alone." After Mama left me and walked toward the office, I never saw her leave the school. I assumed she went to work after she met with Miss Lyons. I was anxious in all of my morning classes and could hardly wait for lunchtime so I could relax and talk to friends. During lunch, while I was standing talking to my friends, I looked up and saw Miss Lyons hastily walking toward me. She said to me, "I need to see you in my office." I was thinking that I was really in big trouble. When we arrived in Miss Lyons' office, she closed the door and remained standing. She looked at me and said coldly, "I want to apologize for telling you that you couldn't sit at the same table with your friends. You have my permission to do so." With that said, she told me I could return to lunch and told me she would see me at the committee meeting after school. She never shared with me the discussion she had with my mother. I could hardly wait to get home and talk to my mother about her discussion with Miss Lyons. I told my mother what Miss Lyons said to me about giving me permission to sit with my friends and how I was not kicked off the committee. My mother's response to me was, "Let's let it go. The situation has been taken care of." I knew not to ask any further questions. The banquet committee did a beautiful job decorating the lunchroom and everyone had a great time.

The last important senior activity was the Senior Prom. I wore a sparkly gold dress, with thin straps. I invited Lee Brothers, the freshman student from Drake University, to be my date. We double dated with another couple. Lee was the nicest guy and looked extremely handsome when he picked me up. Lee was happy to escort me to my senior prom even though he was in college. My father really liked him. He said, "Now THAT guy comes from good stock!" My mother also adored him. For a graduation present, he surprised me by giving me a dainty Bulova watch, with tiny diamonds around the face of the watch. It was the most expensive jewelry I had ever owned. I was reluctant to accept the gift because, to me, it felt like Lee wanted us to commit to a more serious relationship. On the other hand, I could see how happy he looked when I opened up the gift box. We continued to date over the summer, when he didn't have football practice. However, at the end of July, while we were sitting on my front porch, I broke up with him. I told him that I wanted to go to college without any attachments. Lee looked extremely hurt when I told him this. I was worried that I had made a mistake, but knew that college had to be my priority focus. I offered to return the watch, but he told me he wanted me to have it. He got up and walked slowly from my porch. I ran to him and gave him a big hug. That was the last time we dated.

High School Graduation

Everyone in my family was as thrilled as I was on graduation day. My father was especially proud, accepting that I would be attending college out of state. My mother fixed mounds of food and invited all the graduates and their families, black and white, to come to our open house to celebrate. Our house was full of people who came throughout the evening. I was happy that many of my white friends and their families also came.

It's Actually Happening

August 1963 was an exciting time. Dr. Martin Luther's King March on Washington was the most inspirational movement I had experienced. Many people from all ethnic backgrounds walked to our capital to show support of the Civil Rights Movement. I will never forget how powerful and emotional I felt taking that walk to our capital holding hands, singing together "We Shall Overcome." Yet, admittedly, my focus turned quickly to the most important thing for me, and that was preparing to go to college. I received information from the college, updating me on the things I needed to know or things I needed to do. I was sent a long list of books that I was required to read. Two of the books on the list, which I really enjoyed reading, were J. D. Salinger's novel *Catcher in the Rye* and George Orwell's novel *1984*. This futuristic dystopia novel seemed so remote and mystical. It was only 1963 when I read it. Ironically, much of the predictions have come to fruition today. Both books were written for adults; however, high school students later became required to read these novels.

Miss Grace kept in constant contact with me, making sure that I was keeping track of all of the requirements needed for college. I sometimes wondered if she thought I might back out and not attend. I continued to assure her I was following up on everything the college was sending to me. She expressed that she was happy that I was leaving without having a boyfriend to think about. I believe it made her very nervous when I started dating Lee. She reminded me that the reason why marriage was not allowed for a woman who wanted to teach school, was that the focus may not be on teaching the students. I was amused when she told me this again. Knowing how much she wanted me to become a teacher, and not wanting anything to deter me from reaching my goal; I appreciated her caring.

On the last Sunday before I was to leave for school, while at church, our minister asked me to come to the front of the altar. I was so embarrassed, especially knowing many of my friends were at church. Pastor Gaines put his arms around my shoulder and said, "Sister Paula will be leaving for college and we want the members to pray for her." He invited the entire congregation to form a circle around me and pray for my protection from sin and to have God guide me to do well in school. Throughout the prayer, the congregants were saying, loudly in unison, and repeatedly, "Hear our prayer, Jesus." "Thank you, Jesus." "Send your angels before her." I was very uncomfortable, but knew Mama had requested this corporate prayer. After church, I was barraged with kisses, hugs, and tears of joy. I was quite touched with the love that surrounded me.

By the first of September, I was almost all packed and ready to take the Greyhound Bus for a second time to Yankton College. However, this time I was going as a full-fledged Yankton College student. My parents purchased a big black trunk for me to place my clothes, toilet articles, and books. My father wrote PAULA MARIE HEARIOLD in big bold letters on masking tape and placed it on the top of the trunk. Just as I was finishing packing, my younger sister, Kathy, and her friend Delores came into the bedroom. They both were smiling and had a sheepish look on their faces. Each was carrying small duffel bags. They said they had a surprise for me to take to college. They opened their bags and laid out on the bed two Bobbie Brooks A-line skirts, in navy blue and brown; matching sweaters; matching knee-high socks; and three pretty pair of panties. My mind was racing, wanting to ask where they purchased such thoughtful gifts, yet not knowing whether I wanted to know the answer. Both Kathy and Delores stood in front of me, still smiling, waiting for my reaction. I finally, but gently, not wanting to seem unappreciative, asked, "Where did you get these beautiful clothes?" They said in unison, "We got them from Yonkers Department Store." Yonkers was the most exclusive department store in Des Moines and Bobbie Brooks was one the most expensive clothes lines for teens. Kathy insisted that I accept the clothing. "Please take them. I really want you to have some cute clothes to wear while you are at college." Tears filled my eyes; both from heartfelt appreciation, but mostly knowing the risk she and Delores had taken just for me to have nice clothes for college. Had they been caught, they would have been picked up for shoplifting. The worse part would have been having my parents be called by the manager of the department store. My parents would have been extremely humiliated, especially being black, and very angry that my sister shoplifted. Had my parents found out about the stolen clothes, they would have marched my sister and Delores back to the store with the merchandise, asked to speak with the store manager, and insisted that my sister suffer whatever consequences the store deemed necessary for the offense. They also would have been angry at me for accepting the illegal "gifts." In fact, my father would have been so angry that he might have threatened to not allow me to go college. It seemed parents, at least mine, had a lot more control over their children in earlier days, even if they were young adults. My father was a loving father; however, it took him a long time to be forgiving when he felt one of us in the family had done something to disgrace our family. He was always conscientious and talked about the "white man's" distain and distrust for black people. He wanted us to avoid, at all cost, any behavior that would give whites, who he believed were in the authority over blacks. I knew Kathy would be hurt if I didn't accept the clothes she had stolen for me to take to college, and I knew it was wrong for me to keep them, yet admittedly I was grateful that I had new clothes. I carefully packed them and put them in my trunk, without telling my parents. I gave Kathy a big hug; we both cried as we held each other. Somehow I was able to rationalize, unfairly, that it was Delores' influence that made my sister shoplift the clothes. Delores had a reputation for getting into trouble. Blaming Delores made it easier for me to accept what my sister did; however, I knew it was wrong no matter how hard I tried to justify it. I know that there are many people who may think unfavorable of me because I accepted the stolen clothes; however, this act of unconditional love and risk that my sister took to show her compassion toward me; made me overlook the transgression.

Mama insisted accompanying me on the bus ride to Yankton. She knew I would be gone away to college for a long time, and she also wanted to see the campus, my dormitory, and meet my roommate. Daddy also thought it was a good idea. He was already nervous about me going away so far. I was really happy that Mama was coming with me. She and I had never been on a trip alone together. It meant a lot to me, knowing she had to take off work to ride with me. She told me the ladies, whose houses she cleaned, were more than kindhearted; they all agreed to pay her for the three days she would be away. I thought that was really thoughtful. Mama and I had fun laughing and talking all the way to campus. Mama made sandwiches so the only thing we bought during the stopover was soft drinks and potato chips.

As I began reading the mileage posts, indicating we were getting closer to Yankton, I started getting butterflies. Sensing I was nervous, Mama took my hand. As soon as we got closer, the bus driver bellowed, "Next stop, Yankton, South Dakota!" Everyone started standing up and grabbing carry-ons from the overhead. I was wondering how Mama and I were going to get the heavy black trunk out from underneath the bus; Daddy had checked it in for me. Luckily, the bus driver took it out, with little effort. As we walked off the bus, I saw two blue vans, with two men and a woman standing by them. I was happy to see that one of the men was Mr. Green. He walked over to the bus with a big smile; he was looking at a tablet with a list of names on it. He started calling out different names, as each person acknowledged whom they were, he shook their hand and said, "Welcome to Yankton College." When he got to my name, he said, "You are Paula Heariold. I remember talking to you." I was so elated he remembered me. I nodded my head and said, "Yes. I am Paula Heariold." He looked over toward my mother and asked, "Are you Paula's mother?" My mother acknowledged by putting out her hand, "Yes. My name is Dorothea Heariold." Mr. Green shook her hand, warmly, and told her it was nice meeting her. He then said, "Please excuse me. I want to make sure the students know which van to get on." All of a sudden, I noticed that there were not any other parents besides my mother. I became very nervous about Mama coming to campus with me. I didn't think to ask Mr. Green, beforehand, if it was all right for parents to come to campus on the first day. I looked up at my mother and said, "Mama, I don't think you are supposed to come with me." My mother said, hurtfully, with the saddest look on her face, "But I thought the purpose of my coming with you was so that I could see the campus and your dormitory." The woman standing by the van was looking back and forth at the two of us, not knowing what our conversation was about, while at the same time looking somewhat impatient that I was not coming to get on the van. I told Mama that I would be too embarrassed if I was the only student who came to college with her mother. My mother replied, regrettably, that she understood. She hugged me tightly and kissed me on my forehead. She walked back to the bus station. The woman, whom I found out later was a senior on campus, motioned for me to get on the van. Tears were streaming down both of our faces. Mama looked back as she said, "Please call your father to tell him we arrived safely and that I won't be staying." I asked if I could please make a quick call on the payphone to let my father know that I arrived safely. The senior told me to be quick. I regretted making that phone call, not wanting to hear Daddy's response. His reaction was even worse than I thought, "What do you mean your mother is on her way back? I can't believe you had your mother come all that way and then not take her to that stupid campus! I should make you get right back on the next bus and bring your ass home!" Tears were streaming down my face. I was trying to stand with my back turned so I couldn't be seen. All I said was, "Bye, Daddy. They are waiting on me." I hung up the phone. Although the others getting on the van were looking at me, chagrined, they kept their heads down and didn't say anything to me.

As long as I live, I will never forget the sad look on Mama's face. The fragrance of her Channel No. 5 perfume, which was the one extravagance my dad indulged my mother with on every special occasion, still lingers with me. As I look back to that day, I still regret that I didn't tell Mama to come with me on the van. I can still remember thinking about what she must have been feeling as she took the long bus ride back home. I was so naïve and frightened...and stupid.

To my dismay, when I arrived on campus, there were many students with their families, unpacking their cars and carrying boxes and luggage to the dormitory. I wanted so badly to run back to the bus station and get Mama. However, I knew she was gone. Besides, I had no transportation or anyone to take me back to the bus station. The student who drove the van asked two male students, who were walking by, if they could help carry my humongous trunk to the top of the stairs of my dormitory. I was embarrassed for them to see my trunk, especially since Daddy had written my name on the top, with big black letters. As I stood in front of the dormitory, I saw Mr. Green walking toward me. He walked up to me with a big smile, "Hi, Paula. Are you getting all settled in? " He looked around and kindly inquired, "Where is your mother?" I told him that my mother had only planned on coming with me on the bus, but had to return home immediately because she had a very important appointment. I wanted so badly to tell him the truth, but felt he would think my mother was not very kind for not coming to campus with me. I did not want to prolong the conversation so told Mr. Green that I was anxious to pick up my room key and begin unpacking my trunk.

My mind shifted to how awesome it was going to be to see Betsy, seeing someone I had already met so I wouldn't feel so lonely. When I arrived at the housemother's living quarters, she introduced herself and told me how happy she was to meet me. She was a very kind woman, very short. She spoke in a very soft voice, and displayed a half-smile. Her eyes had dark circles around them, as though she needed more sleep. She directed me to a box of keys and told me what room number would be attached to the key. When I entered the room, Betsy and her parents were already in the room. She and I literally screamed with excitement, as we jumped up and down, hugging each other. Betty's parents were busy putting on pretty matching sheets, with a matching bedspread on her bed. They had already decorated the room with bright posters. Betsy, trying to get their attention, said, "Mom and Dad, I want you to meet my roommate." When they looked up from the bed, Betsy said excitedly, "Mom and Dad, meet my roommate, Paula." She continued, "Paula, my parents, Dr. and Mrs. Stuber (pseudonym)." Both parents looked startled and certainly not happy to meet me. It was at this point that I realized Betsy had not told her parents that I was black. Betsy's mother made an inaudible comment and scurried out the door. In a few moments, the housemother came back with Betsy's mother. She said, "Paula, I am so sorry, there's been a mistake. I told you to take the keys for the wrong room." Betsy looked furious at her parents and belligerently shouted, "Paula and I agreed to be roommates when were together during College Weekend. We both received our room assignments this summer with each of our names on the room assignment sheet. There is no mistake!" Betsy's mother asked me to step out of the room so her parents could talk to the housemother, which I did. After the housemother came out of the room, which seemed forever, she told me that I would be assigned another room. She seemed completely unsettled by the whole matter. I held back my tears and wanted desperately to run back to the bus station and go back home with my mother. The housemother told me that the whole situation would be resolved, and that I would be staying in her quarters for the first night. I was so humiliated and hurt. The next day the housemother told me that I had been assigned to another room with a very nice girl. She took me to the room and introduced me to Marjorie. Marjorie came from New York and had an accent similar to Betsy's. She seemed happy that I was going to be her roommate. Marjorie was a little different in that she was somewhat abrupt and came across a little jerky. In spite of her quirkiness, she was very sweet and had a great sense of humor. The two of us got along well; although socially we didn't do much together. I knew that I needed to meet other students to socialize with so I wouldn't be labeled strange by just hanging around Marjorie. Some of the students had already begun to make fun of her. I was too insecure by not laughing along with the other students when they made fun of Marjorie; still, I didn't feel good that I didn't defend her.

Betsy apologized to me about how her parents treated me. I said to her angrily, "Betsy, why didn't you tell your parents that I was black? You must have known that they don't like black people!" She said to me, "I thought once they met you they wouldn't think of you as being black. I talked about you all the time and my mother knew how excited I was that we were going to be roommates." I couldn't believe how gullible Betsy was, thinking her parents would be oblivious to the fact that I was black. She told me that her parents loved their black housekeeper and the nanny who took care of her and her sister when they were young. We were both hurt and disappointed over the situation. It reinforced for me, that no matter what, being black would always be a divisive factor among most white people. I remained friends with Betsy; however, I didn't feel quite the same toward her as I did when we met during College Weekend.

It didn't take me long to adjust to campus life. There were a few students who made fun of my grammar, which really embarrassed me. It took me awhile to get my pronoun and verbs to agree. Mostly all my friends and the families I grew up with in my hometown of Iowa said, "She don't, he don't, and it don't." My diction was not the best. I would pretend I wasn't offended and would laugh along with the students when they said I talked funny. However, I made a chart for myself and kept it on my desk so I could practice correct grammar in my dorm room. I was determined to speak the same way the white students spoke.

I loved Kingsbury Hall. It was a magnificent three-floor colonial brick building, with stairs surrounding the wide veranda. All the meals, except Sunday, were held in the dining hall, which was located in the lower floor of Kingsbury Hall. Many of the students hung out on the veranda after dinner. It was also the place where a lot of flirting took place. I wasn't quite sure where I fit in, since I was the only black student who hung out with the "cool" popular East Coast girls on the veranda after dinner. I always cringed when I sensed the conversation moving toward a racial discussion. The Civil Rights Movement was in full swing throughout the rest of the country during this time. It seemed as though protesting was prevalent on every major campus; however, no protesting took place on our campus. I don't believe there was a lot of empathy toward the plight of black people; all students, including me, lived in our own little bubble at Yankton College.

Kingsbury Hall dormitory

When a male visitor arrived to pick up a girl at Kingsbury Hall, a student receptionist would buzz her room. My friends and I would giggle and peek downstairs to see who had come. The visitor was asked to wait on the other side of the foyer, which was a large sitting room on the other side of the receptionist desk. It was decorated like what I imagined looked like a British Queen's Headquarters. There was a gigantic Turkish red carpet that covered most of the entire dark wood floor, two large lamps with maroon tassels around the lampshades which sat on round antique tables, placed strategically at the end of two big maroon brocade chairs, separated by a matching brocade couch. I loved sitting in the "waiting" room. I pretended that it was my living room. Although my living room at home was a pale comparison to the "waiting room." I so hoped that my dorm room would get buzzed, alerting me that I had a male visitor whom I could visit with in the beautiful sitting room. Marjorie would laugh and say, "The only way our room will get buzzed is if the housemother wants to see us."

I had developed close friends among some of the girls in our dorm. Three or four of us would gather in the other one's room smoke cigarettes and gossip about the boys on campus. We enjoyed playing pranks on some of the other girls in our dorm. One Sunday evening, since dinner was not served in the dining hall, a group of us talked about how hungry we were, but really didn't feel like going out. I actually didn't have money to eat out anyway. I recalled that Mary, who was a music major and not very popular, constantly received boxes of food from home. One of the girls suggested that we raid Mary's room for food while Mary was at the Conservatory Hall rehearsing for an opera concert. We sometimes cooked soup in our popcorn poppers, which was against house rules and forbidden to do so in our rooms. It was decided that we steal soup and crackers from Mary's room. When we heard Mary coming, I quickly greeted her at the hall entrance and invited her to join the other girls and me in my room to share soup. Mary, who was the floor monitor, was responsible to report to the housemother if any of the house rules were broken. However, Mary was so elated to be invited to eat with us, since she had never been invited before, that she agreed to break the forbidden rule. We could hardly eat, without laughing, watching Mary eat her own soup. Mary continued to tell us how fun it was to be together and that she would like to invite us to have soup in her room one Sunday evening. To this day, I am still ashamed of the unkind prank we played on Mary.

There were three very nice and good-looking black male athletes who attended Yankton. All three were juniors. Jesse was on the football team, Dave was on the basketball team, and Tom was on the track team. Since they were "jocks," they were very popular on campus. I developed a friendship with all three of them. Jesse and Tom were already dating girls on campus so I decided I would vie for Dave's attention. One evening when Marjorie and I were in our room studying, our buzzer went off. We both jumped up as though we were hit by lightning. When I answered the in-house phone, the receptionist let me know that I had a male visitor. The other girls, who already peeked down the stairs, were saying excitedly to me, "Oh my God, it's Dave, the basketball player. He's coming to see you!" After looking in the mirror and putting on lipstick, I slowly and nervously walked down the winding steps where Dave was standing at the end of the stairs, smiling, which unnerved me. My first thought was, *why didn't he go into the "sitting" room and wait for me?* He greeted me and asked if I would like to go to the snack bar with him. We walked to the snack bar and had a good time getting acquainted. Dave continued to visit me at the dorm. It seemed that we both enjoyed spending time in the "sitting" room talking. I begin attending all of his basketball games, and waited for him after the game. We walked around campus, holding hands, and spent hours talking in the student lounge. We became one of the most popular couples on campus. He, like I, did not have much money so he was not able to take me out to dinner or to movies. All the girls thought it was so cool that I was dating Dave, the "star" basketball player. No one seemed to mind that Jesse and Tom's girlfriends were white, since both were also star athletes. Dave and I continued to date almost the entire semester. I was surprised that my dad permitted him to drive me to my home one weekend. Dave seemed to "hit if off" with Daddy right from the beginning. He slept on our couch in the living room. Daddy stayed downstairs with Dave until I went upstairs to bed. Dave and I really endeavored to be boyfriend and girlfriend, but realized that our dating was for the wrong reason. Our attraction to one another was based on him being a star basketball player and that both of us were the few blacks on campus to date. Neither of us had that "heart-throbbing" feeling towards each other. Dave shared with me that he wasn't really into dating white girls and was happy when he saw me on campus. We broke up, but remained friends. My girlfriends in the dorm continued to probe, "How could you two break up? You looked so cute together."

A Rude Awakening

The campus was picturesque. It sat on a beautiful rolling hill. Everything looked so fresh and green, with vibrant leave colors of red, yellow, and green. The winter brought snow that covered the entire campus, making everything appear fresh and clean, just as I felt my life had become. I believed I looked so studious, carrying my books, as I walked around campus. As studious as I may have looked, I was not doing well academically. I had never learned how to study and continued to have failing grades in most of my classes. At the end of the first quarter, I had a .9 G.P.A. I was totally humiliated and did not let any of my friends know how poorly I was doing. A letter was sent to my parents (that's when parents actually were sent information regarding their college student's academic standing), alerting them that I was being placed on academic probation. The letter stated that I could not return to college if my grades were not improved by the end of the semester. My father was furious, accusing me of going away to college just to "mess around" when I could have stayed home and had a good job. The Academic Dean met with me to reinforce that I was in jeopardy of losing my scholarship and that I would not be able to attend Yankton after the first semester if my grades did not improve substantially. I cried so hard that snot was running down over my lips. I kept wiping my face with my forearm. The Dean took his handkerchief out of his pocket and gave it to me. After I stopped shaking uncontrollably, while crying, I told the Dean that I didn't understand most of the test questions and didn't know how to study. I also told him about Grace and how disappointed she was going to be that I "flunked" out of college. Grace had already begun to return each letter I sent to her with big red correction marks circled around misspellings or incorrect grammar. At first this made me really angry and I told myself that I was not going to send her any more letters, but then I began to realize that she was just trying to help me. The Dean told me that if I promised to go to the Study Center every night, from 7-9 P.M., that he would assign a tutor to help me study. He said to me, "This will mean your social life will be on hold until the end of the semester." I agreed to this commitment. However, I told him that I also was supposed to work in the library, a work study program, assigned to me three nights a week, which was helping pay for expenses not covered by scholarships. He said, "Let me deal with that, you just focus on getting your grades up." I had already made up a fib by telling my friends that I didn't really like Yankton very much and that I may transfer to another college at the end of the semester. This was to save face just in case I was told that I could not return. My partying days decreased significantly. I spent most of my spare time in the library. I also begin studying with other students, something I had not done before, because I was afraid to show my ignorance. I met with professors when I didn't understand a problem. I learned that asking questions showed that I was inquisitive, and did not mean that I was dumb. By the end of the semester, with a great amount of help from my tutor and focusing on the areas for which I should study, my G.P.A. was raised to a 3.0. I told my friends that I changed my mind and decided to stay at Yankton.

While in high school, I thought I was academically prepared for college and I became livid as I looked back at the clement way my teachers showed no regard for my learning. They really didn't have high expectations for me or any of the other black students as long as we came to class, was polite, and quiet. I received A's whether I understood the work or not. I don't recall ever really being challenged. White students, who took proficiency tests and scored high, were placed in college preparatory classes. I don't remember ever being given a proficiency test to see if I qualified for advance placement classes or of having been encouraged by my guidance counselor to do so. Many of the college-bound white students received ACT tutoring throughout high school, the test that was given in Iowa rather than the SAT, to show colleges that a student is academically prepared for college. Although I took the ACT test, I scored low in all four sections of the test. Yankton College, in its quest to recruit minorities, accepted me because of my high school G.P.A. I graduated from high school not having the skills I needed to attend college. The reality of being faced with the deficiency of my academic skills made me feel insecure and out of my league, which, admittedly, I was. I went from graduating from high school feeling intelligent to entering college being totally ill prepared. I was outraged. I entered college with maladroit college preparation skills. Neither of my parents attended college. My mother graduated from high school and my father went as far as the 8th grade. Where Daddy grew up, in Keysville, Missouri, there was not a high school for black students to attend. Although all of my sisters were very intelligent, none of my older sisters were encouraged to attend college. I did not grow up in a college-focused environment.

Life on Campus

By the end of my freshman semester, I began to feel a bit more confident. I worked on improving my diction and increasing my vocabulary. Grace, who was my guardian angel, continued to return all my letters with big red circles, correcting misspellings and grammar. I was proud of myself when I noticed that there were fewer and fewer red marks that Grace sent back to me. I actually looked forward to receiving Grace's corrections and found them to be endearing. I was touched by the way Grace wanted to help me succeed in college. I developed close friendships with four of the girls in the dormitory. They were all from the East Coast and were relatively wealthy, at least by my standards. What I found really amusing, given all the expensive clothes the girls wore, two of the girls loved my Bobbie Brooks outfits and were constantly asking to borrow one of them, which made me feel delighted that they would want to borrow clothes from me. I never revealed how I acquired them. Borrowing each other's clothes was quite common among the girls in the dorm; however, I never felt comfortable asking if I could borrow anyone's clothes and never did ask. These new friends were completely different from any of the girls I had grown up with. I had never known anyone who had come from New Jersey, New York, or Pennsylvania. In fact, besides my white high school classmates, I never had an opportunity to build genuine relationships with white girls. My dorm friends and I got to know the East Coast boys pretty well, by hanging out on the veranda after dinner. The East Coast boys had their own unique look; generally they wore navy blazers, madras shirts, khaki

pants, and penny-loafer shoes, with no socks. I thought they looked really cool. My dorm friends and I spent our weekends hanging out at the "Ice House," a place where beer was delivered to the car, similar to a drive-in restaurant. The Ice House waiters came to the car to take orders and brought beer directly to the car, just as they did at the A&W Root Beer stands. I.D. was only requested from the driver of the car, even though everyone in the car was drinking beer. I was only seventeen when I first started college so I placed correction tape to remove the last number on my birthdate and then retype, with precision, the earlier date I pretended that I was born. I was surprised how original the updated birthdate looked. I felt pretty special that I was included with the "cool" group of kids. Afterwards, we went to a place called Tommy T's Bar to dance and listen to music.

When the girls and I returned to the dormitory, we would gather in one of our rooms and talk about which of the boys we thought was really "hot" and which ones we thought were nerds. Eventually, the matchmaking began to happen where each of my girlfriends were paired up with one of the East Coast boys. We still all hung out together until the end of the evening, which is when I said goodnight and returned to my room to talk to Marjorie, my roommate. Marjorie seemed to live vicariously through my social life. She was always interested in hearing about my evenings hanging out at the Ice House and Tommy T's Bar. Marjorie generally stayed in the room, seldom venturing out on the weekends, except to go to the library. Eventually, she became friends with Fran, another shy girl who lived down the hall from us. Fran also did not have a social life. I was so happy that Marjorie found a close friend. I sometimes would go to a movie with the two of them when the other girls were on a date with their boyfriends.

One evening when my dorm friends and I were hanging out talking to the East Coast boys, I noticed that one of the East Coast boys was really flirtatiously looking at me. I pretended that I didn't notice and, animatedly, continued to laugh and talk. As my girlfriends started pairing off with their boyfriends, I decided that I would leave for my room. Just as I was about to say goodnight, Bill (pseudonym), one of the boys who wasn't dating any of the other girls, stopped me. He said, "Why are you leaving so soon? Why don't you come with me to the Ice House?" I smiled, not sure if he was just being nice to me or if the invitation met more than that, and said, "Sure." He and I got in the back seat of his friend's car. My girlfriend looked at me, sneakily, as she got in the front seat with her boyfriend. That was the beginning of Bill and me liking each other, yet not committing to each other that we were more than friends. It was my first time having "feelings" for a white boy. Several times after that first time in the car together, we would talk when not many people were around. I saw my other dorm girlfriends walking hand and hand with their boyfriends while they were walking around campus. I wasn't quite sure what my relationship was with Bill. We never really talked about it. However, we did kiss when we were alone. After the first kiss, I shared with my dorm friends that I really liked him. We always would giggle and tell each other our "secrets." One of my close friends inquired, "You guys make a cute couple. Why doesn't Bill come and sit in the lounge with you ever?" Having guys ring their girlfriends' rooms to just come to visit them was common. I was a little uneasy when she asked me this question. I was thinking she was telling me that maybe Bill didn't like me the way I liked him. I found that she was right. Yet, Bill and I continued to have our escapades. However, it was becoming clear to me that when we were with friends, Bill was not as open about showing his feelings toward me. I also intermingled with friends, masking any feelings I had toward Bill.

One day I got up the courage and walked over to Bill while he was talking to a group of guys. I just wanted to see his reaction. He acted as though he didn't know me. He looked irritated at me, as he continued to talk to his friends. He looked as though he wanted to tell me to leave; actually he looked as though he didn't know me at all, even though I had hung out with him and his friends several times. I didn't understand his behavior and was embarrassed about the way he was treating me. I walked back to my dorm, devastated. I shared my feelings of disgrace with a few of my close dorm friends. My dorm friends said they didn't know why he treated me this way and felt sorry and sad for me. I believed I had made such a fool of myself for even thinking he would be interested in a black girl. I made a vow that I was never going to speak to him again. One day, as I was walking across campus, Bill was walking directly toward me. I put my head down and tried to walk by him as quickly as possible. He stopped me and said, "Paula, wait." I looked up at him and said, "Don't you ever speak to me!" He told me that it was important that I listen to what he had to say. I stopped, still very angry. He said to me very slowly, "I didn't know how to handle my feelings for you. I had never dated a black girl before and, admittedly, I was embarrassed when you walked up to me." He continued, "I know now that I was wrong." When he finished talking, I said to him, disdainfully, "You should have thought about that before playing with my emotions. You humiliated me publicly by treating me as though I had leprosy!" He continued to attempt an apology; I kept walking. I was so hurt and peeved with myself for allowing myself to get involved. For some reason, I thought race relations were different at college. How soon I had forgotten about my first roommate's parents and how her parents didn't want their daughter to room with me. I had become too comfortable in my college setting, thinking that being black was no longer an issue. I had let my guard down and should have known better. Interracial dating was taboo and not accepted, especially by most white parents. From that time on, Bill and I were both uncomfortable when we were hanging out together with the East Coast group. I was not aware if any of them knew what happened between Bill

and me, or if they were aware that we had even been together alone. Bill and I made eye contact several times, while we were out with friends. Speaking with our eyes: I knew we both still cared for each other. Bill left school and returned back to Connecticut at the end of the semester. I pledged that I was never going to allow myself to be put in this situation again, especially by dating a white boy.

It never dawned on me to ask my parents how they may have felt about my dating a white boy. I believe my father would not be too pleased; but eventually may have accepted him once the guy "proved" himself to be worthy of me. It was a moot discussion since I chose not to tell them about Bill, nor did I tell them about the ordeal about how Betsy's parents treated me when her parents found out I was assigned to be Betsy's roommate. I cannot imagine how my mother would have reacted if she had been with me when Betsy's parents went to the Dorm Mother to tell her it was not acceptable for me to room with Betsy. I envision my dad would have told me to "bring my butt home" and continued by repeating what he had said before, "I told you that you should never have gone to that college in the first place." Just when I was beginning to feel comfortable in my black skin; reality set in that I would never have equal standings alongside my white friends, no matter how close we became. I was still black.

Losing My Hero

Daddy just weeks before he died

Istayed at college during the summer of my freshman year. I worked as a waiter at a summer resort so I could make extra money. Another student, Ana, from Venezuela, also stayed that summer and worked at the same resort with me. After work, we came back to the dorm and emptied our apron pockets to see who had made the most tips. The men, who came in for drinks in the evening, seemed creepy to Ana and me. They used to flirt with us, saying things like, "You two little Indian girls sure are pretty." They didn't have a clue what ethnic background we were from and we didn't bother telling them. Ana and I would smile kindly, knowing we would get more tips if we innocently batted our eyes at them. This was as much as they were going to get from us, with the exception of the food we were serving them.

One afternoon while Ana and I were working, I noticed Tom, our boss, coming across the lawn, walking with his head down. I knew in my heart that something was wrong. He walked over to me and said, "Kiddo, I need to speak to you." I followed him outside. He said to me with a serious look on his face, "Your grandmother is on the phone and needs to speak to you. You can speak to her on the phone in my office." He told me he would wait outside until I finished my conversation. I remember being in a daze, not really wanting to take the call. I knew that something bad had happened, not knowing if it was about my mother or one of my two sisters, who still lived at home. I was not prepared for what Grandma Brown said to me. I was not even sure I heard her words clearly. "Your father died," she said softly. For some reason, I didn't think that the bad news would be about Daddy. He was bigger than life! He was invincible! I don't even remember asking what happened to Daddy or hanging up the phone. Tom came in and put his arms around me, as I stood in a trance. Tears flowed down my face, but I was too much in shock to cry audibly. My grandmother had already told Tom what had happened. Tom didn't have to ask me about what my grandmother said to me. I didn't know what to do next. How was I supposed to get home? Tom wasn't sure what I was supposed to do either. I believe he thought my grandmother told me what to do. My mind was swirling. I thought to myself that I should call Mary, one of my friends whom I stayed in contact with over the summer. Mary lived on campus during the school year, but she was from Yankton. I occasionally would spend the night at her house during the summer. She came from the nicest and most caring family. When I called Mary to tell her my dad died, she immediately yelled to her mother, who was outside gardening, to tell her what happened to my dad. Mrs. Bormann, Mary's mother, came in and took the phone from Mary; Mary's mother told me that she was coming immediately to get me from my job. When we arrived at Mary's house, her mother quickly began making phone calls. I had no idea who she was calling, but the calls sounded very official. The next thing I knew she told Mary to pack a few clothes because Mary would be escorting me to my home on a plane to Iowa. I wasn't even aware that Yankton had an airport. I found out this was a small private airport. I was nervous about having to fly on a plane since I had never flown on a plane before, but knew I had to get home and felt less nervous since Mary would be coming with me. Mrs. Bormann drove me to the dormitory so I could pack my clothes. The next thing I remember was that Mary and I were boarding a small plane, heading for Iowa. To this day, I don't remember if other people were on the plane or who met Mary and me at the airport. What I do remember is seeing how sad my mother was. That's when I began to cry uncontrollably, as I held my mother tightly.

I still think back about the kindness that Mrs. Bormann showed by making all the arrangements for me to fly home and how sweet it was for Mary to accompany me, without even questioning her mother about why she should. Mary and her family met my family only once, and that was only a couple of weeks before Daddy died. It was quite brave for Mary to accompany me home and fly back alone, especially under such dire circumstances. Her family's unwavering support spoke volumes about the sheer kindness of their family.

It was almost as if Daddy had a premonition before he died. He decided two weeks before his death that he wanted to drive my mother and sisters to visit South Dakota to see the college campus and me. It was so unusual for Daddy to plan a trip at the last moment. He always had to have everything all planned out. I was so happy that my family came. I was excited and proud to introduce them to my boss and the people at the resort. It was important to me that the people at the resort see a respectable and classy black family. Many of the local people in Yankton had never, personally, met or talked to a black person, until I started waiting tables at the resort. My dad was so handsome and my mother very beautiful. They weren't loud, but spoke gently, just as they had taught us to act around white people. Yet they were both very genuine and kind. I wanted to show the local people that this was not your stereotypical black family. My family demonstrated elegance, even though they were common laborers. I walked them all around the resort, introducing them, "Hi, Tom. This is my mom and dad and my two sisters, Kathy and Dorothy." My dad, with a broad dimpled smile, responded, "Nice to meet you. Paula has enjoyed working here this summer. I am glad she is working with such nice people." Mama put her hand out and nodded with agreement with what my father had said. Daddy showed interest in the resort by asking how long the resort had been operating and asked Tom how long he had worked at the resort. Tom, looking a slight bit uneasy engaging in a conversation with my dad, not expecting him to inquire about the resort, responded, "This resort has been here for over 25 years. I was their original manager. The man who bought the property wanted someplace for visitors to come when they came to Yankton (he chuckled), but to be honest most of the locals come since we don't have a lot of out of town visitors." Daddy replied, "Well, now you have visitors from Des Moines, Iowa." My face hurt from smiling so hard as I looked up at Daddy. I was so proud of him.

We had a great time. Daddy even splurged and took us out to what we thought was a fancy restaurant. It was the last time I saw him. He died of a massive heart attack at the young age of 42 years old. He was my hero! I wanted to make him proud of me by being the first member of our family to attend college. He was such a wonderful father and worked laboriously to provide for our family. He and I were very close. I give my father credit for modeling and exhibiting the exemplary traits of what an outstanding father and man should be. I looked for these same traits in my relationships with men I dated and what I desired in a man with whom I would marry. I believe the stress of being the only black employee under such pressure to do well, not to speak of the racism he encountered, took a toll on his young life. I remember him telling me that "Being the 'only' does not mean not being the best." That phrase has stuck with me.

Home Girl

I convinced one of my best friends, Robby, to join me during my second year of college. She applied and was accepted. Even though I had met many friends at college, it felt really wonderful to have a black friend, with whom I could culturally relate. The most urgent concern that Robby and I had was how to deal with our kinky hair. Robby and I obsessed about keeping our hair well groomed. This was of utmost priority. Prior to Robby coming to school, during my first semester at college, I met a black couple at the downtown supermarket (the only black couple in town). I boldly walked over to them and introduced myself. They introduced themselves as Mr. and Mrs. Miller. I told them my need to have someone wash and press my hair. Mrs. Miller kindly said she would be happy to help me. She agreed to pick me up from time to time, when she was available, if I called to let her know when I needed my hair done. I wanted to say, "NOW!" We agreed that the following week would work for both of us. I told Mrs. Miller that I would rather meet at the supermarket than on campus. She told me that they were not able to drive into town very often, being that they only had one car. However, Mrs. Miller said I could come to her house if someone could bring me. I certainly did not feel comfortable asking one of my dorm friends to drive me to the black family's home. I knew that even though Mrs. Miller charged very little, I still had very little money to spare so would not be getting my hair done often.

I arranged to see Mrs. Miller at the supermarket two weeks after we met. I got up early that Saturday morning and quietly got dressed. My roommate sleepily awakened and inquired, "What are you doing up so early? It looks like you are getting ready to go out." Usually on Saturday mornings we slept in and walked down to breakfast together. I mumbled something like, "I need to get something from the supermarket." I said to myself, "Don't be so damn nosey!" I quickly hurried out the door before Marji could ask me more questions. Mrs. Miller was waiting at the supermarket when I walked in the store. I did not know what to expect when I entered her home. She had a very small quaint home. I could smell a pot of lima beans cooking. I knew the smell because it reminded me of the smell of Grandma Brown's lima beans that she cooked on most Saturdays. I wondered if Mrs. Miller would be making homemade cornbread to serve with her beans. Mrs. Miller must have been reading my mind because she said, "I have some lima beans cooking. They should be done by the time I finish your hair if you would like to eat some before you go back to your dormitory." I told her I could not stay for dinner because I had to get back. She then offered to send some with me, which made me delighted. I could heat them in my popcorn popper and have them for Sunday dinner. Mr. Miller came in from another room, smiled warmly and greeted us, then immediately left the house after we walked in. I got the impression he didn't want to be around while Mrs. Miller was washing and pressing my hair. Washing and drying my hair was a laborious process. It was painful holding my head down in the sink while Mrs. Miller washed my hair and then poured a pan of water over my hair, which ran down my face and into my eyes. When she towel dried my hair with a big towel, my hair turned into a humongous looking bird's nest.

I returned to the dorm with a scarf on my head. I quickly ran to my room before anybody could see me. I assumed my roommate would be gone. She went to the library on most Saturday mornings. I frantically tried to brush my hair out and restyle it. I was happy that it was washed and pressed, but didn't like the way it looked; besides it was way too oily. One of the girls walked in my room, "Where were you? What did you do to your hair?" I was annoyed with her questions and the fact that she burst into my room, without knocking. In most cases, I would not have cared, because we walked into each other's rooms often, but this time I was uncomfortable with her seeing my hair before I could restyle it. I believe my friends began to recognize that I was uncomfortable with their probing about my hair; they eventually stopped questioning me regarding my disappearing escapades. Dealing with my hair was a major pain!

It was such a blessing when Robby came to college, besides being good friends, we could help each other with our hair. We decided that we would have to learn how to do each other's hair and not try to get our hair done at Mrs. Miller's house. We knew that it was going to be an arduous feat to do our own hair, but had no other choice if we wanted to get our hair straight. We definitely worked hard at mastering the craft of doing our own hair. Ironically, our white friends did not understand this whole ritual that Robby and I went through, since all they had to do was wash, towel dry, and put gigantic rollers in their hair. Robby and I dreaded the thought of getting our hair wet when we got caught in the rain or when students thought it was funny to have water fights. This would throw us into a major panic.

We were so ecstatic when my mother sent me an electric hot comb. Robby and I would wait until most of the girls left the dorm, usually on a Sunday afternoon, when many of the girls were studying at the library or were hanging out with their boyfriends. We would go to our room, lock the door, wash each other's hair in the sink, blow dry it, and then straighten each other's hair with the hot comb. This procedure created smoke in the hall and gave off a pungent smell of burning hair. The process included, pressing our hair with the hot comb, sectioning pieces of the hair, putting a touch of gel on the ends, and rolling up the hair; hoping when the process was complete, we would have a nice pageboy that looked similar to our white friends. We would giggle quietly when we heard some of the girls, who returned to the dorm, say loudly and disgustedly, "Yuck, it stinks in here. It smells like something is on fire!" One of my Armenian friends, who had kinky hair, found out what Robby and I were doing to our hair. She asked, "Can I join you in your secret? My hair is kinky too. Could you guys also straighten my hair with your hot comb?" It was comforting that one of our white friends experienced the same challenge we had with our hair. Sadly, Robby and I believed that in order to "fit in," our hair needed to resemble that of the white girl's hair. We made sure that our hair was "presentable" at all times. It became exhausting!

Robby was very popular on campus. She became instant friends with the East Coast gang that had become my friends. Robby joined us in our favorite pastime. Over the weekends, we did the usual; we sat in someone's car and drank beer and then headed down to Tommy T's Bar to dance. This was our typical Friday and Saturday night ritual, just hanging out with groups of friends. Robby and I were the only blacks in the group. With the exception of my hurtful experience with Bill, it was easy to temporarily forget about our racial differences; we all had so much fun together. Before Bill left for home, I finally became a little more comfortable being around him when we were in a group together. Even though there was flirting that occurred between other boys and me, I made sure that flirting was where it ended.

Robby met a very nice guy named Lenny. They became chummy friends during one of our outings. They began walking to class together and talking together, after dinner, on the Kingsbury veranda. Lenny was from New Jersey. He fell "head over heels" for Robby. Robby also became very attached to Lenny. They walked to class together and met up after dinner. They were very happy. However, when Lenny's parents became aware of Robby being black, as well as not being Jewish, the relationship ended. It was a painful break-up for both of them. I believe they might have gotten married, if race and religion had not been a factor. Unlike Bill, Lenny was not ashamed to let the entire campus know how he felt about Robby.

Robby and I became independent of each other by developing individual campus friends. Still, it was very comforting having a close friend from home attending college with me; someone who was ethically and culturally connected. We were able to share uncomfortable racial situations we encountered, sublimely and overtly. Many of our East Coast friends transferred to larger colleges on the East Coast after the end of our second semester of college. I no longer hung out at the bars as much as I did my first two semesters of college. I began to focus on my major, which was secondary education. At this point I knew that I wanted to be a secondary English teacher. I no longer felt like the young "green" college student. I was aching to graduate and become the first person in my family to become a college graduate, as well as become a teacher, just as Grace had predicted.

College Graduation

The last two years at Yankton College seemed to soar by. I loved attending college at Yankton. I cherished the friendships that I developed over the years and the beautiful South Dakota seasons. The winters brought snow that covered the entire campus. There were always fun snowball fights and laughter. I loved the crackling fire that burned in the living room fireplace at Kingsbury Hall. When spring arrived, small blossoms began to crop up, reminding me of my new beginnings, as I looked forward to graduation.

My life at Yankton College had been attending classes, studying for exams, hanging out with friends at Tommy T's Bar, laughing (lots), and being happy. I don't recall ever watching the news or reading a daily paper. However, the first and most memorable moment was on November 22, 1963, my freshman year. I recall sitting in American Literature class when one of the administrators came to share the terrible news about the assassination of President Kennedy. We were all stunned and devastated by this horrific news. The campus closed and students returned home to share Thanksgiving with their families. I believe everyone wanted to be home to grieve together. This was the first time I became aware of how uninformed I was about what was happening in the outside world. My focus had been about my intellectual and emotional growth while attending college. My voracity for learning overshadowed my need to know what was going on outside of my bubble. There was a sense of protected isolation at college. I was completely unfettered by the tumultuous crisis that was occurring everywhere in our nation.

As graduation neared, I began to realize that my protected bubble was going to burst.

I spent my last semester student teaching at Yankton High School. In the beginning, I could see that the students were somewhat uncomfortable having me teach their English class; however, it did not take long before they warmed up to me. I introduced African American novelists and poets into the curricula. The students appeared to be thirsty to learn more about African American literature. I was pleased that my supervising teacher was more than delighted that I was teaching about authors she had not known about or included into the curricula. The students were very open and sincere about wanting to know more about me and what it was like growing up black. We had great discussions about race and culture. I liked that the students felt safe to speak to me about their personal stereotypes regarding black people and how some had never met a black person before. These were discussions that I had never had with my white friends during college. Was it a topic we felt uncomfortable discussing or were we so alienated from what was happening outside of Yankton that we truly did not think about our differences? In my case, I certainly would have never shared my insecurities nor talk about how guarded I was, watching my every interaction so as to not appear stupid. I had never encountered the same experiences as my white friends. They talked about participating in such activities as taking English riding lessons, vacationing in Europe (to some places I had never heard of), and having an extra home on the "shore" to go to during summer vacations.

As my student teaching assignment came to an end, I realized how much I really enjoyed teaching. The students presented me with an album, about me, that included poetry. Every student from all three of my English classes wrote a poem about me. I had no idea how they pulled off such a beautiful surprise. I was told that the students worked on the album before and after school. I was really touched by their kindness and was elated that I had such a unique experience, teaching all white students and making such an impact. The principal, who was extremely kind and warm, offered me a teaching position for the following year. He had observed my classes several times. I was honored by his offer, but was ready to go back home, among family and friends of color.

I was so excited on graduation day. Mama was making her second trip to Yankton on the Greyhound Bus. This time, I was going to make sure that she saw my dormitory room and the entire campus. While students were bustling all around, I took a cab to meet Mama. As she stepped off the bus, she looked so elegant and beautiful. When she embraced me tightly, I smelled the delightful aroma of her Channel No. 5 perfume. She flashed her amazingly warm smile, highlighted by her flawlessly straight pearly teeth. Her lips were perfectly outlined with radiant bright red lipstick, and her soft brown curls bounced gently as we walked toward the cab. I don't believe my mother realized how stunningly beautiful she was. I was so proud of Mama when I introduced her to my campus friends. They also commented on how pretty she was. My childhood feelings returned, wondering if they were asking themselves why we looked so different because of my darker skin and kinky hair. This question oftened entered my head when I was with Mama around white people. I walked Mama all over campus and showed her my dorm room. I wanted her to see everything she had missed when I didn't know if she was supposed to come with me my freshman year, a painful thought I had tried not to remember. She was greeted warmly by several of my friends' parents and was invited to sit with them during the ceremony. This made me happy since no other member of my family was able to attend.

As we lined up to walk across the stage to be ready when our names were called, I honestly thought I was going to faint. I was so nervous! I thought, almost out loud, *Why did I wear these high-heeled shoes that I can barely walk in?* All the other students looked so giddy and calm. I couldn't believe this day had come. My eyes filled with tears, which I tried hard to hold back. My thoughts turned to Daddy. I wanted so badly for him to be at my graduation. I could just hear him telling his Friday buddies, "I have to go and see that hardheaded girl of mine graduate from college," knowing how exceptionally proud he was, but pretending it wasn't a big deal. I also could hear his friends saying, "George, you know you can't wait to see Paula walk across that stage," laughing hardily while they passed the bottle of Jim Beam around in the brown paper bag. I also reminisced about Grace and how much she influenced me in my decision to attend college and how she coached me all along the way. Miss Grace had promised, my freshman year, that she was going to be at my graduation. A promise I believe she made to make sure that I stayed in college and graduated. Sadly, Miss Grace had become very frail and was not able to attend. When I called to tell her about the ceremony, she responded to me, in her very weak voice, "I know you are going to be the best teacher ever. I am so proud of you!" I told Miss Grace that I had made a commitment to carry on her legacy. That was my last communication with Miss Grace. Before I knew it, I heard in a loud, boisterous voice, **"Paula Marie Heariold!"** That was my cue to walk across the stage. I was so elated that Mama was there to see the first person in our family receive a college diploma, with the class of 1967.

Yankton College was the pivotal point in my life. I met lasting friends with whom I continue to stay in contact. I realized, while attending college, that color, ethnicity, and culture, even for a season, appeared irrelevant as I became intertwined with building sincere relationships and getting to know other students on a personal level. I learned how to focus and to develop a love of learning. I found that I was able to attain what I once thought was unattainable.

A Passion Fulfilled

I was so proud to receive a document in the mail that stated that I was certified in the State of Iowa to teach secondary English. Ironically, my first teaching assignment was to teach high school English at the same high school where I graduated. It seemed strange and almost embarrassing to teach students who were only a couple of years older, some who were friends with my two younger sisters. It also seemed uncomfortable to become colleagues with teachers whom I had taken classes with while in high school. The demographics had changed since I was in high school. The school was mostly minority students. However, all of the teachers were white, not unlike when I was attending North High as a student. Many of the students seemed not to care about learning and the teachers didn't seem to care if they learned. I wasn't sure if some of the students took me serious, as a teacher, or just viewed me as one of kids in the neighborhood. I never felt at ease going back to my high school to teach. I could tell immediately that this teaching experience was going to be completely different than the one I had while student teaching the high school students at Yankton High School. I had left Yankton High School feeling so optimistic about teaching; now I was not so sure I was in the right field.

After the first year of teaching, I requested to be transferred to a junior high school. Surprisingly, I was assigned to teach at my former junior high school. The principal, Mr. Spriggs, was black and the majority of the students were black, unlike when I attended. I was impressed that high standards and expectations were what were expected from the students.

My first teaching job

The students seemed to take pride in their learning. Teachers challenged the students and developed professional relationships with the students. The students had respect for their teachers because they knew that the teachers and the administrators sincerely cared about them. Many administrators and teachers identified with the students and had traveled the same journey as they. I was proud to be a black teacher, teaching minority students. I felt that I was making a difference in their young lives, knowing that for many, when they left school, they would be faced with many challenges beyond their control. School was a safe haven. I loved introducing the students to classic play writers and authors they had never heard of before. They loved writing haikus and acting out plays. I enjoyed entering the classroom every day. Miss Grace was right; I had found my love of teaching. I put my heart and soul in teaching my students. I considered each one my students a "merchant of hope." Just when I thought things were going so well, I was faced with a huge dilemma. The vice principal, who was white, took a serious liking to me. In the beginning, I thought he was a really thoughtful administrator who was giving me support. I had total respect for him as the vice principal. I began to feel uneasy when he started coming to my room often and would sit in the back of my class room. I questioned him, "Are you concerned about my teaching? I seemed to be getting observed a lot." He said, "No, as a matter of fact, I just like your style of teaching." His response gave me an uneasy feeling. He then started coming into my classroom after school. I was a new teacher and did not want to make accusations against him that would jeopardize my job, but was still nervous. He was highly respected by the principal and the other teachers, which made me not want to say anything to anyone for fear they would think less of me. Before I knew it, rumors started buzzing all around the school that I was having an affair with the vice principal. This became a big deal, not just because he was the vice principal, but also because he was white, which was even a bigger deal than the fact that he was married. I finally, but gently, shared with the vice principal (whom I will call Mr. T.) that rumors were spreading around the school that we were in a relationship and that I was feeling uncomfortable about our friendship. He smiled, "So let them talk. I want us to be together. I told my wife how I feel about you." He told me that his wife wanted to meet me. Everything turned so creepy. I told Mr. T., "I don't want to be in a relationship with anyone who is married." I realized that what I said didn't really get my point across. I didn't have the courage to tell him that I wasn't interested in him and that I wouldn't want to date him even if he wasn't married. I never was good at being completely truthful if I thought it would hurt someone's feelings. I remember in college going out with some nerdy guys just because I didn't want to reject them like other girls had done to them. Then I had to wiggle my way out when the guy(s) wanted me to go out with him again.

What made me really sad was that my students had begun to treat me differently. This made me feel really terrible. One of the students asked, "Miss Heariold, are you going to marry that old white man? Why he keeps coming into our classroom?" I also believed some of the teachers had begun to distance themselves from me, especially the black teachers. I had a very close white friend, whom I taught and graduated from high school with, that sympathized with me. She could see this situation exploding before her eyes. Not too long ago, during one of our high school reunions, she shared with me that she saw how Mr. T was stalking me and wanted to report him. The weird thing was that I was so naïve that I didn't look at Mr. T as stalking me. In fact, I felt guilty, as though I had done something wrong. Was this my entire fault for being too friendly? Did I act or say something to encourage him? I probably was not giving him the "message" that I was uncomfortable with him. I believe had he been black, I would have been more comfortable being forthright. I actually felt bad for the vice principal, yet I didn't know how to stop the wreckage. I was horrified when Mr. Spriggs called me into his office, on a Friday after school. I did not realize that the vice principal had gone to Mr. Spriggs to share his feelings about me. Mr. Spriggs point blank inquired, "Miss Heariold, are you having a relationship with the vice principal?" I swore to him that I was not. He responded by saying, "Well, in that case, I will be asking for his resignation. After all, he is your supervisor and should not be harassing a teacher." I didn't know what to say. I could read a look of disgust on Mr. Spriggs' face. I imagine that Mr. Spriggs felt betrayed by Mr. T., whom he had liked so well. I think he felt betrayed by Mr. T. attempting to have an affair with one of his young black teachers. Mr. T., in my eyes, wasn't really harassing me, yet as a mature adult and one who has been a school administrator, I would have made the same decision as Mr. Spriggs. The following Monday Mr. T. was not at school and never returned again.

Tumultuous Year

I had accomplished my goal of returning to Des Moines, as a schoolteacher, and living in the same town with family. However, my dashing hope of happiness with a teaching career and connecting with family had been shattered. The experience at the junior high left me reeling. In addition, my mother was stressed and worried about my two younger sisters, who were not attending school and were pretty much out of her control, both running with the wrong crowd and getting high on drugs. I constantly worried about Mama, who had been an energetic healthy person, and now was challenged with diabetes and high blood pressure. Mama appeared immobilized, barely having the emotional or physical energy to do much. Her joy was limited to talking on the phone with her lifelong girlfriends, which made me happy to see and hear. I enjoyed seeing her broad, wide smile return, as I watched her laughing heartily during her long conversations on the phone talking to her best friends, Laura and Evelyn.

I was not prepared to encounter how much had changed since I went away to college. It appeared my corny little Iowa town had completely fallen apart. Male friends whom I had known almost all of my life were returning home from Vietnam. Many of them had been injured. Some did not return at all. Drugs were rampant, especially among black males. Many overdosed and died from heroin. There was not an outcry of concern in our hometown or in the country about the high number of drug deaths or use of drugs among black men, quite the contrary. In fact, the demise and epidemic was looked upon from the vantage point of sheer disgust for the street "users" and how they had become a menace to society, as well as to our community. There was a total lack of compassion for this horrific drug disease among underrepresented populations of young men and women. I began to understand the reason behind the discouraged critical state of affairs among blacks, especially black males. There appeared to be an overwhelming cloud of despair. Although my father and his friends were not drug users, I remember seeing this look in my father's and his friends' eyes; I saw it in the eyes of the black kids I taught, and I saw the same look in the eyes of the black, young and old, people, who stood aimlessly on street corners, seeming to be completely incapacitated by their futility of life. I felt when I walked past them, they looked at me with distain, as if to say, "Who do you think you are? Looking all uppity." Or maybe that was the guilt I was feeling, as I walked by them. Perhaps they were looking at me with envy. While growing up I, like the others, received the same subliminal message from white privileged people; the message that we were not "as good as." I continue to allow this subliminal message to creep into my head, but continue to block it, knowing I had been blessed by receiving support and encouragement from others, like Miss Grace. I possessed the true grit to move forward. I learned that other blacks may not have had the same make-up or support as I received. I have diligently worked on not judging others who have been less fortunate than I, which guiltily I have done in the past. I had begun to be more realistic, coming to grips that no one comes into this world deciding that he or she is willingly not going anywhere in life. Although my heart is filled with compassion, at the same time I feel displeasure, wanting so much more for my black sisters and brothers.

While attending college in South Dakota everyone seemed to have goals and were looking forward to a bright future. I had lost touch with reality. I didn't feel a sense of belonging. I had a difficult time re-assimilating into my own culture. Some of my friends, whom I had known since we were kids, alienated me. Some made accusations by telling me that I had changed since I returned home from college. They would ask, "Why are you acting so white?" One of my friends, whom I had been really close to from grade school through high school, asked, "When did you start talking so proper?" I felt in many ways that I had become disconnected from my own race. There was a part of me that wished I had gone to a black college and joined a sorority where I could have celebrated black sisterhood. However, that wasn't my choice either. I observed many black sorority women and fraternity men become snobbish toward other blacks. I called this the graduated "Jack and Jill" elite. I was torn, feeling anger and frustration toward the inequities and prejudice toward blacks, yet, feeling annoyed that what appeared to me, was a number of blacks wallow in their self-defeat rather than try to improve their status in life. I, admittedly, felt guilty thinking like this, knowing the obstacles many of them faced.

The Civil Rights Movement, which was motivated by such activists such as John Lewis and Dr. Martin Luther King, gave me a great sense of pride, seeing black people become more courageous to stand up for equal rights. I also was encouraged to see sympathetic white people support the Civil Rights Movement. I found myself somewhat of an outlier, wanting to be engaged in the movement, yet not feeling comfortable becoming an activist. I had become too comfortable living in my bubble, encircled by privileged white friends. In spite of Dr. King's "dream," there continued to be a festering of anger and hate emitted between blacks and whites. Many black people were not "experiencing the dream" of freedom and equality; they were becoming impatient with Dr. King's strategy of the use of nonviolence to bring black and white people together. Dr. King's dream was losing steam and was not the effective strategy that so many had hoped for. I remember watching Dr. King on our little black-and-white television screen, observing the discouraged look on his face, and hearing the strain in his voice. I heard his unwavering strong plea as he appealed to everyone to keep working toward peace, love, and justice. Hearing his arousing speech, I could not help but ask myself, "Why is this so difficult to achieve?" The very next day, April 4, 1968, Dr. King was assassinated. Shot dead at only 39 years old. People around the world were grief-stricken and in shock. I was stunned and felt physically sick the entire day. Dr. King was such a strong civil rights leader who lost his young life fighting for all humanity. After the assassination, there was even more anger among blacks. Riots erupted in black neighborhoods in every city. I didn't understand why blacks were destroying their own communities, but began realizing it was misplaced anger. "Burn, Baby, Burn" was an angry outcry of a reaction to injustice and racism.

Two months after Dr. King was assassinated, Senator Robert Kennedy was assassinated on June 5, 1968. I felt as though we had lost the only white leader who really empathized with blacks, regarding their inequitable station in life. I could feel my own anger well up as I also began to lose hope and trust that racial relationships could ever be resolved. The relatively harmonious relationships that I had with many of my white friends became strained. I became increasingly aware that it seemed that our racial differences were much too ingrained to overcome. In spite of this feeling, I maintained friendships with many of my white friends. I thought if I could build a relationship between my close white friends and my close black friends, they would begin to know each other on a personal basis, as I had experienced in college. One evening I invited two of my white male friends, who lived in my apartment complex, and one of my black girlfriends to attend a dance that was hosted by a black community group. The moment we walked in, I could feel the unfriendly stares. I knew right away that I had made a mistake. Two black males, who were known to be troublemakers, walked up to the two white males and punched both of them in the face, unprovoked. I was horrified, as well as angry. I felt responsible for what happened. I was surprised by one of the comments one of my black friends made to me. She said, "You should have known better than to bring these guys here." She went on to say, "You're beginning to act like you are white." Her comments were hurtful. I felt shocked that no one stepped up to defend my two white friends. We left the dance, with blood dripping down both of the guys' faces. My girlfriend and I knew that there was nothing we could do to make the situation better. Surprisingly, the two guys said they understood the assailants' anger and begged me to let it drop. It was difficult for me to face the two guys for some time. The sting of racism remained very raw.

Sam Cooke's song, which he composed in 1964, "A Change is Gonna Come," seemed to be a prelude to the reshaping of America. Singers like James Brown were singing songs to inspire blacks to take pride in their blackness. His song "Sing It Loud, I Am Black and I'm Proud," was heard daily on the radio and on "boom boxes" throughout the black community, even young kids were singing the words to the song. The song became the black mantra. The Black Panthers' Movement became a significant force among many blacks. Continued oppression and hopelessness seemed to contribute to the support of the Black Panther Party. Angela Davis, who was among one of the most influential political activists, shunned the "straightened hair" look that so many black women spent hours in beauty salons, having relaxers to "straighten" their hair. Ms. Davis demonstrated her black pride by letting her hair go "natural," which became known as the Afro. Women, children, and men sported Afros. The bigger the Afro, the more emphasize on black pride.

I did not feel comfortable wearing an Afro. Part of me wanted to remain an individual or not draw attention to myself, not feeling secure enough to outwardly showcase my blackness. Another part of me was that I did not want to distance myself from white friends. These perplexing times left me feeling completely flummoxed, tense, and somewhat fearful. I felt emotionally drained and torn, losing who I was and, not knowing who I was to become. To quote Charles Dickens, "It was the best of times, it was the worst of times." I was literally experiencing being pulled between two worlds. Although there appeared to be no end to these tumultuous times, there seemed to be a spirit of love and hope brewing among the chaos. Song groups like Peter, Paul, and Mary, as well as Simon & Garfield, were singing songs of love and peace. The racial unrest, however, did not feel that it was going to change anytime soon.

Navy Blue Suit, White Blouse,
and High-Heeled Shoes

I knew that I was ready for a new environment—a new place where I could redefine myself. A friend, who worked for IBM, shared that the company was hiring school teachers to train new customers on the use of IBM equipment. I applied immediately and was "over the moon" to receive a call inquiring if I could come in for an interview. I was so nervous wondering what would be their reaction when I walked through the door for the interview. I wondered if I should call before my interview and say, "By the way, do you know that I am black?" I thought to myself that *would really be a ridiculous question.* How would they respond? "Oh, in that case, don't come in." For a fleeting moment, I thought about cancelling the interview and just stay in my teaching position at the junior high school. After all, the vice principal was gone and maybe things would go smoother once school started. I got a horrible pit in my stomach, just thinking about going back to the school and all the drama it caused. After my nerves calmed down and I was overcoming my anxiety, I decided to go in for the interview and give it my best shot. The day before the interview, I went to Younker's Department store, Mama's favorite place to splurge when buying my sisters and me a birthday gift. I bought navy blue pumps, a navy blue straight skirt, white blouse, and even new underwear. I went to Miss Betty June's hair salon to have my hair pressed and styled in a pageboy. When I walked into the interview, I was pleasantly surprised to be greeted by an attractive black woman. She was so warm and elegant. She put out her hand, "Hello, Miss Heariold, Cynthia Turner (pseudonym). I work out of the regional office in Minneapolis." Just seeing her made me instantly relaxed. "Please call me Paula, Miss Cynthia." She smiled, "I also am comfortable having you call me Cynthia." I thought to myself, *She must think it lame calling her Miss Cynthia like she's some old lady.* She definitely was not an old lady; she was the most sophisticated black woman I had ever met. I wondered how she got such a "kick-ass" job. We chatted about my college experience and my teaching position. I believe she was impressed when I told her I attended college in South Dakota. She said, "That can be an advantage working at IBM" She didn't expound on why she made that remark, but I surmised it was because she believed that I would know how to act around white people. She explained what the position would entail and told me that the job would not be located in Des Moines, explaining there were openings in several cities and that Des Moines did not have an IBM Office Products Division for which this position was hiring. "How do you feel about leaving your hometown?" Little did she know how thrilled I was hearing that there was a possibility for me to move from Des Moines, Iowa. Nonchalantly, without wanting to act overly zealous, I replied, "I would be fine with that." My interview lasted over an hour. Miss Turner told me I would be receiving a response within the next couple of days. I was thrilled, yet filled with fear when I received the call from Miss Turner. I honestly could hardly comprehend what she was saying to me. "I called to offer you the position." Was that what she really said? Was I actually being offered a position with IBM, one of the most prestigious companies at the time? It was coined "Big Blue," perhaps because everyone wore blue suits. I was especially happy that the new position was located in in St. Paul, Minnesota. I thought of myself as replicating the life of "Mary Tyler Moore," even though she was white and lived in Minneapolis. She seemed to have such an exciting life. I even wore my hair in a "flip" like she styled her hair. I loved that T.V. show.

I offered my resignation to Des Moines Public Schools. I felt somewhat guilty leaving behind the students whom I believed I had encouraged in so many ways, not just in academics, but also about making healthy choices, and keeping their focus on attending college. I loved teaching my students and tried, daily, to instill in them that the color of their skin or being poor did not define who they were. Unfortunately, I knew that this wasn't necessarily easy, given the many obstacles I had encountered, however, I did not want them to give up. It was my desire that they could see me as an example of who they could become. They and I had come from the same environment and shared many of the same obstacles, yet I was fortunate to have the opportunity to see another side of life. It was a hard decision, leaving my students; however, I knew that the time was right for me to begin a new lifestyle with a fresh beginning, and in a different city. So many of the people I knew and grew up with appeared "trapped" and did not seem to have the courage to leave what they saw as their safety net. I felt the need to personally say goodbye to Mr. Spriggs. I knew there would be very few people around since it was summer. I somehow wanted him to know that I was sorry about what happened with the vice principal. For some reason, I never stopped feeling somewhat responsible that Mr. T. had lost his job, especially knowing that Mr. Spriggs and he had a good relationship, prior to my coming to teach at the junior high. Luckily no one was in the office, not even the secretary. I knocked softly on Mr. Spriggs' door. "Mr. Spriggs, do you have a moment?" He looked at me bewildered, but nodded for me to come in. I clumsily fumbled, trying to find the right thing to say. "I just want to thank you for hiring me. I loved teaching here and appreciated your support. I didn't feel I could pass up the experience when IBM offered me a good position. Besides, I thought it was a good time to leave Des Moines. I wanted to resign early to give you time to hire a new teacher while it's still summer." There was a pregnant silence before Mr. Spriggs replied. "Miss Heariold, I appreciate your coming in. I wish things could have turned out differently; however, I wish you luck with your new position." He dismissed me without saying goodbye, but by turning his attention to the papers on his desk. I thought it better just to walk out the door. I left with a big knot in my stomach, feeling I had really let Mr. Spriggs down, yet not knowing what I could have done differently to prevent the embarrassing and unpleasant situation that I endured while teaching at the junior high. My guilt continued to linger; I was a young black teacher whom, I believe, many thought had enticed a white married man to fall in love with me, and caused him to lose his job.

IBM offered to reimburse me for all of my moving expenses, as well as pay for a moving van to move all of my furniture. I found this somewhat amusing since I did not have much to move. I had a couch, chair, small table, and a wooden dresser, all of which I purchased from Goodwill. My small apartment included a Murphy bed that I, hurriedly, pushed into the wall anytime someone came to visit. My sister, Connie, and her husband, Donald, volunteered to drive me to St. Paul. My mother looked forlorn when she walked me to the car. Later, Mama shared with me that she was going to give me a twenty-dollar bill she had tucked away in her apron pocket but thought it was such a meager amount that she was too embarrassed to offer it to me. Connie and I laughed when I told her what Mama said about being embarrassed to give me the twenty dollars. We could have used the money. Connie and I only had ten dollars each, which was just enough money to buy White Castle hamburgers, French fries, and milkshakes for the three of us. I was pretty broke after sending my first monthly payment to live at the YWCA, which I had arranged before I left Des Moines. I also paid off the bills I incurred, for clothes and shoes that I bought, that I thought necessary for my new professional business look. My final, much needed check from the school district was to be sent to me at the end of the month. I chose to live at the YWCA since I knew it was close to the office and thought it would give me an opportunity to meet other women, not knowing anyone, with the exception of three of my close family friends who lived in Minneapolis and were also new to the area. One of the first women I met was Dorothy. We became instant friends. Dorothy was challenged with Cerebral Palsy. She had a great sense of humor and was a lot of fun. I believe we "clicked" since we were both different from the other women who lived at the "Y." The other women didn't seem to reach out to either of us.

I was so nervous the first day of my new job. Rain was in the forecast and I was paranoid about my hair getting wet, especially since I had it pressed, curled, and styled in a very neat page boy the night before I left town. "Lord," I prayed, "please don't let it rain!" As I sat on the bus on my way to the office, thoughts and questions kept swirling through my head: *Do I walk in with a big smile? No, don't come across overly gushy! Will someone be there to greet me when I first arrive? What if I screw up? Walk in with confidence and remember to offer your hand first. Please remember to use correct grammar!* I was wearing my new navy blue suit, white blouse, and navy blue high-heeled shoes. My friend who told me about the position told me that this was the IBM "uniform."

When I arrived at the IBM building and entered the elevator, I was so relieved that I was the only one on the elevator. My heart was beating rapidly. I was trying to calm myself by taking slow deep breaths. I didn't realize that when the elevator door opened, the office was immediately facing a reception-ist. She greeted me with a warm smile and offered me to take a seat. She said, warmly, "Mr. Miller (pseudonym) will be out shortly." Mr. Miller was the Branch Manager. My nerves began to settle down. Mr. Miller came out of his office and walked over to me with a beaming wide smile. I quickly jumped up and held out my hand and said, "Hello, Paula Heariold." I said this, so quickly, before Mr. Miller could even hold out his hand and introduce himself. I could feel that I made this an awkward moment, feeling I had screwed up before I even got started. With that, we skipped the preliminary introductions and Mr. Miller proceeded to tell me how happy he was that I had joined IBM He warmly said, "Let me show you around and introduce you to the rest of the team." Everyone was gracious and welcoming. I learned that I was not only the second woman to join the team, but also the first black person. All my in-securities returned, asking myself, "What if I do not measure up to what is ex-pected of me?"

Judy, the other female support representative, made me feel very comfort-able. She had only been on the job for a few months; however, she seemed so confident and self-assured. She was cute and perky, I could see that she already had built a strong rapport with the salesmen by the way she, so slightly flirta-tiously, laughed and causally talked to them. She walked me in the training room and showed me the computers we would be training customers on. It was apparent, by the way she demonstrated the various uses of the equipment to me, that she had become competent in knowing how to use the applications and was prepared to go out to conduct training in the field. I spent the first week reading the training manuals and observing Judy teaching classes when customers came to our training room. The second week, a sales representative named Dan was assigned to me. He was to give me direct hands-on training. Dan was strikingly tall and distinguished looking, wearing a pinstriped navy blue suit, white shirt, and highly polished black shoes. I was seated in the train-ing room when he arrived. I smiled up at him, but I didn't receive the same response from him. He was all business. He stood over me, which was very unnerving. He spoke very quickly as he began to point out different areas of the equipment and their functions. I asked him politely, "Could you please slow down a bit? I need a little more time to grasp what you are teaching me."

I was shocked when he said to me in an annoyed voice, "I don't understand what you don't get!" There was so much to learn about the equipment and the applications. I began to feel completely over my head. The information he was teaching me was coming at me like bullets hitting me in the head. I was so over-come with anxiety that I could not, comprehend what was actually being said to me. It was as if he was speaking to me in a different language. I was thinking, *How humiliating this is going to be if I don't grasp these concepts. The first and only black person hired for this position, who is incapable of doing the job.* I became emo-tionally and physically distressed. I informed the sales representative that I needed more time to read the manuals. I honestly was ready to run out of the office and never come back. As I fought back the tears, I thought about the struggles my mother and father had endured and how their resiliency gave them the confidence to not give up. Daddy taught me independence. I had learned, from him, his unyielding courage to not give up, in the face of hard-ship. I stayed in the training room, after the salesman walked out, and began looking over the manuals. Mr. Miller came in the room. "How you doing?" he inquired. I responded, with as much composure as I could drum up, "I am doing great (exaggeration), but need a little more time to go through the training manuals." He smiled and said, "Take as much time as you need. There is a lot of information to digest." I felt proud of myself for being honest and not faking that I was ready for hands-on training. I decided that I was not going to beat up myself for not knowing everything immediately; ho-wever, I told myself that I was going to, with a vengeance, become proficient in learning the applications as well as Judy, if not better. Judy made me feel even better when she told me it took her more than a week to grasp most of the concepts of the applications, and that she was still learning as she was teaching. I was beginning to become more acquainted with the other sales representatives in the office and was able to "small talk" with them, while at the same time not wanting to become too familiar with them, protecting my-self from what I had experienced with Mr. T. at the junior high school. One of the sales representatives, named Jerry, was very nice to me. I was feeling more confident about my knowledge on the use of the applications. Jerry sat beside me in the training room and listened and watched me as I demon-strated to him how to use the equipment, just as if he was a customer. This was so helpful and gave me even more confidence.

IBM was manufacturing more and more new applications for their computers. The sales representatives, along with Judy, were sent to Dallas, Texas, for additional training. Mr. Miller informed me that I also would be sent for training, after I had mastered the fundamentals of the computer. I was still on probation so it was important that I received high marks when I went to IBM training, which would determine whether I would remain an I.B M. employee.

The training was for two weeks; it was fast moving and strenuous. People from IBM offices all over the country attended the training, yet I found myself to be the only black person attending. My fear of failure returned, knowing the pressure I would be under to compete. It appeared that the other attendees were making a concerted effort to meet each other. They were going out to dinner, and having drinks at the end of the day. I thought about asking to come along, but it seemed just too difficult for me to make the effort, fearing rejection. Many of the trainees met in the evenings to practice with each other on what they would be demonstrating to the group. I went to my room and practiced by myself, in front of the bathroom mirror. As I look back, I ponder if perhaps, not knowingly, I was sending negative vibes, causing others to not know how to include me. I believe I made the white trainees uncomfortable around me, since I was not making them feel comfortable by overtly being outgoing and reaching out to them first, which is expected from some whites. Each day we were expected to go in front of the entire class and demonstrate our knowledge on the use of the applications. All eyes were on each of us when it was our turn to demonstrate. When it was my turn, I felt as though I stuck out more than anyone else. The reality was that everyone else in the class, in all likelihood, was just as nervous.

During the third evening of the training, I began experiencing serious heart palpitations. I felt as though I was having a heart attack. I decided I should take a taxi to the emergency room at the general hospital. It seemed as though I sat in the emergency room forever before finally being called. When the doctor came in to see me and checked all my vital signs, he informed me that everything was normal. He told me that, based on my symptoms, it appeared that I was suffering from an anxiety attack. This was the beginning of my serious onset of Anxiety Disorder, which I still experience today. The doctor told me to breathe slowing into a brown bag the next time I found myself experiencing another attack. He suggested that I not take myself so seriously. Easy for him to say! I was surprised when several people from the training heard that I had gone to the hospital. They seemed genuinely worried about me. I told them how much I appreciated their concern. I informed them that my illness was nothing serious and that I had been diagnosed with a mild case of the flu. There was no way I was going to tell anyone that I was diagnosed with an anxiety attack, much less tell them that the doctor told me to blow into a brown paper bag! The empathy that was shown toward me from others in the class made me feel much more comfortable toward the other trainees and gave me more courage to share my nervousness. Not surprisingly, they shared they were feeling the same way. I began to relax and feel more secure about getting up in front of the group to demonstrate my understanding of the new applications. At the end of the two-weeks' training, I was rated "exceeds standards." My confidence soared. I was really proud of myself and felt prepared to give customer training.

When I returned to the office, everyone congratulated me on my success. Even Dan, the salesman who made me so nervous during my first week on the job, said, "Way to go!" I believed this was his way of making me feel better after our first encounter in the training room. My first customer training took place at our office in our training center. Four women attended the class. It was an all-day training session. Larger firms would request group training, which would consist of four to five people. I worried about the training the whole night, but woke up feeling more at ease. I thought back on my first day of greeting students, when I taught school, and decided I would use the same format to get this class started. I had everyone introduce themselves and tell everyone something unique about her or himself. This was not only a good icebreaker for the customers, but was also a way for me to calm my nerves before I began the training. One of the trainees was black. Our eyes connected as she walked into the room. She smiled widely. I knew that she was feeling a kinship toward me, which made her also more relaxed. Blacks have a way of talking to each other with one's eyes, letting each other know that we understand how they are feeling in a majority white group.

The training went exceptionally well. By the end of the day everyone was laughing and talking. The four women worked together on the applications. I observed that they developed even a closer bond than when they came into the room. I detected that the black lady, who was the only black in her firm, became more relaxed throughout the day and was more casual around her colleagues. I was emotionally drained, but was very pleased with how well the training went. Mr. Miller told me that the customer client reported that the secretaries came back very excited about their training. I was feeling that I was being recognized for my work and stopped feeling so insecure about being the only black.

I was really surprised and pleased when Dan came to me and said, "I would like to have you train a customer on one of my very prestigious law firms." I responded by saying nervously, "Are you sure you should not take Judy since it's such an important account?" He said, "You have had the same training as Judy and did well in Dallas." Not wanting him to think I was not prepared, I responded, "Yes, of course." That evening I pondered over whether I should wear my black suit or my navy blue suit. I decided the black suit, accompanied with a crisp white blouse, would look more professional. I arrived at the office promptly at 7:30 A.M. so I wouldn't be a minute late meeting Dan at 8:00 A.M. We small talked while we drove to his account, but kept our conversation on a very professional level. I am usually the chatty one who will ask questions that aren't too intrusive, safe questions, like where did you grow up? However, I could tell that Dan was pretty private so I sat quietly in the car. He shared with me that St. Paul was a very Irish city and ultra-conservative. He went on to say that the law firm we would be visiting had been around for a long time and was somewhat stodgy. I was not quite sure why he felt the need to share this information, but figured he was trying to tell me, without saying it, that St. Paul was not the most progressive city. I hadn't had an opportunity to really get to know the city since I usually returned to the "Y" and met Dorothy for dinner. On the weekends, I did laundry and kept current about keeping updated on the IBM applications, wanting to make sure I understood every aspect for training purposes. I spent every other Saturday getting my hair done at a black beauty shop that the receptionist at the "Y" recommended. Knowing where to get my hair done was one of my top priorities when I arrived in St. Paul, it was as important as knowing which bus to take to the IBM office.

When Dan and I arrived at the law firm, an older bespectacled gentleman greeted us, in the front office, somewhat rushed and not especially friendly. He was the principal attorney. This was an account Dan had for a long time. The law firm was upgrading their IBM applications on their computers and the attorney wanted his personal secretary to have additional training on-site so she didn't have to leave the law firm. Dan introduced me to the attorney as the person who would be conducting the training. He told the attorney that I was very experienced on the new computer applications and that he was sure that his secretary would be pleased with the training she would be receiving. Dan inquired if the attorney could introduce me to his secretary. The attorney stammered and said, "Dan, before I introduce Miss Heariold to my secretary, I would like to speak to you privately." With somewhat of a crooked smile, he told me to help myself to coffee and to have a seat in the front office. This request made me uncomfortable, not knowing why the attorney didn't take me back to his office to meet his secretary. I noticed that the receptionist at the front desk kept her head down as if she didn't want to look at me. This was not the first time that I encountered this unwelcoming environment, and it was not a good feeling. I picked up a magazine, turning the pages, but not really paying attention to what I was looking at. I crossed and uncrossed my legs several times, probably looking as though I had to use the restroom. A few times the receptionists looked up but quickly put her head back down when our eyes met. I asked myself, *what could Dan and the attorney be discussing for so long? Perhaps the wrong equipment arrived.* I could feel the tension when Dan walked out of the attorney's office. He was visibly upset and said to me, "We need to return to the office." I was confused, but got up quickly and followed behind as Dan walked briskly out the door. My instinct told me not to ask any questions. Dan opened the door for me, which he didn't do for me when we left the IBM office. I sensed something unpleasant was said in the attorney's office. Dan pulled his car over to the curb. He looked at me embarrassed as he shared with me, angrily, "The attorney requested to have another Educational Support Representative to do the training." At first I didn't quite understand what he was telling me, then perfectly understood. Pretending to be naïve by not wanting Dan to feel bad, I asked, "Did the attorney want someone with more experience?" Dan, refusing to let the attorney off the hook, vehemently responded back to me, "That Bastard, very pointedly, told me that he did not want a Negro person to do the training!" He went on to say that the attorney told him, "I have too many important clients who come to my firm." These comments reverberated in my head. I did not know how to respond. Dan told me that if the firm did not accept me do the training, then the firm wouldn't be receiving any training from IBM I told Dan that I didn't want to do training at a place where they chose not to have a black person. He responded back to me curtly, "That attorney doesn't have the privilege of requesting who does the training, and you don't have a choice as to where you are requested to train!" I said to him meekly, just wanting to acquiesce to the attorney's request, "Don't you just think it would make things easier if Judy did the training rather than make waves?" He said sternly, "That's not going to happen!" We rode the rest of the way back to the office in complete silence. When we walked into the office, Dan went directly to Mr. Miller's office. The next thing I knew, he picked up his briefcase and walked furiously out the door. I felt responsible for what had happened. It seemed to become a pattern for me to take responsibility when I was involved in situations where there was racial tension.

The dreaded wave of insecurity returned. I hated going to work the next day. I didn't want to face the branch manager or Dan. I could feel the chill between the two of them. I felt like all eyes from everyone in the office were on me. I spent most of the day in the training room, working on customer accounts. I didn't really want to talk to anyone. Judy sensing something was wrong came into the training room, cheerily talking nonsensically to me. I faked a smile as I tried to respond to her in kind. Judy sensed that I was not in the mood for small talk and said she had to get back to a project she was working on. I was curious if the branch manager would assign Judy to do the training at the law firm, especially since it was such a big account. Just as I was deep in my thoughts, I almost jumped out of my seat when the branch manager came through the door. He walked over and sat down beside me. He said, "I am sorry about what happened yesterday at the law firm today, but you must know that there are times when we must make concessions when working with these big accounts. I hope you don't take this personally." I couldn't believe my ears. I thought he was coming to tell me he was sorry about the way the attorney responded by not wanting me to train at his law firm, but what he really was saying is that IBM couldn't afford to lose a big account because of me. His comments had nothing to do about him feeling sorry about the way I was treated because I am black. He put his hand on my shoulder and walked out. I felt like telling him to take his slimy hand off my shoulder. I sat filled with rage. I wanted to run out of the office and give him my resignation right then. Resentment came over me, as I looked at every white person working at their desk, I wanted to scream loudly, "You will never know what this feels like! It's damn hard, trying to pretend that I am not hurt, much less insulted." Knowing better not to say what I really wanted to say, I went into the restroom to pull myself together. I was so relieved when it was time to leave the office for the day. I walked out, trying to be as pleasant as possible, telling everyone to have a good evening. It was cold and gray outside. The bus seemed to take forever to get to my final bus stop. For some reason everyone on the bus looked mean and unfriendly. I began to question why I left Iowa to come to such a gloomy place. After talking and laughing with Dorothy, I felt much better. I woke up the next morning feeling more refreshed, knowing I had to put on my happy face and "brush off" any negative feelings that I harbored the day before.

I was somewhat stunned when Dan came up to me and said, "I apologize for the way I talked to you." He said he was very upset with the attorney who refused to have me do the training and took it out on me. I really didn't want to discuss this incident anymore, but at the same time, I wanted to inquire so badly about how the firm was going to get their training after purchasing so much equipment. I thought better to not ask. That afternoon, Judy suggested we go out for lunch; she shared with me that the branch manager called her in his office to tell her that she would be training at the law firm. Then she told me she was confused because she said, "Dan came to me and told me that I would not be doing the training. He said it had nothing to do with me; it was that he was not allowing the law firm to dictate to him who he should bring to do the training." Judy continued, "Something bad must have happened when you and Dan went to the law firm." I knew she was trying to solicit information from me. I believed she knew more than she let on. I could feel that tension-filled conversations were going on all morning; both Dan and Judy were in and out of Mr. Miller's office. I also knew, by the uncomfortable looks around the office, that I was the topic of discussion, without being included.

Unbeknownst to me, until I found out later, Dan was so upset that he called Ms. Turner at the Regional Office to report the contentious meeting that occurred at the law firm. He also told her how Mr. Miller was willing to send another support representative to appease the principal attorney rather than lose the account. This was a bold action for Dan to take, which ultimately could have cost him his job. It was not looked upon lightly for a subordinate to go directly to the Regional Office with a complaint. It was obvious by the constricted tone of Mr. Miler's voice that he was angry as he announced to the sales team that Ms. Turner was coming to the sales office from the Regional Office the next day. I guess he felt it was necessary to let us all know that "a big wig," as he called it, when someone was coming in from the Regional Office. I was not aware of why she was coming, but was happy that I was going to see her again. When she came in, she was strikingly and elegantly dressed. She had an air of pure professionalism. She smiled warmly, but still had that strong "I am all business" look. She came over to my desk and said, very formally, "Paula, I would like to take you for a late lunch after my meeting with Mr. Miller." I replied, "Sure (nervously). I will be in the training room when you are ready." I quickly went to Judy, "Why do you think she wants to talk to me?" Judy replied, rather rudely, "I don't know, but I don't like being intertwined with all this chaos." I curtly responded, "Why do you think this has anything to do with you?" Her comment irritated me because this made me know that she knew more than she was telling me. She mumbled, as she was walking out of the room, "This could have been resolved without the drama."

When Cynthia came out of the Branch Manager's office, she carried herself with the same warm demeanor while still sending the message, "I am in charge" look. She made a point of walking around speaking to each of the salesmen. Asking each one how they were doing and even personalized her brief interactions by asking about their families. She said to one salesman, "Didn't I hear that you just had a new baby?" The salesman proudly responded, "Yes, we had a baby boy. His name is Nick." The salesman seemed pleased that she was so personable. She commanded respect by the way she carried herself. I pondered what they thought about her being black. After she made her rounds, talking with the salesmen, she indicated to me that she was ready to go to lunch. I felt proud walking out the door with her, yet a tinge of uneasiness with us both being black. I had no idea what our lunch conversation would entail, which also made me apprehensive. As soon as we got to the restaurant and sat down, I could feel a warm connection with Cynthia. "So, how's it going? I would like for you to be honest. I am aware of the entire incident that happened at the law firm. " I thought to myself, how honest should I really be without sounding like I was complaining or not grateful about my job? Yet I didn't want to brush the whole ordeal over, like it didn't make me feel bad. Cynthia got right to the point, "Under no circumstance should you or anyone else be subjected to racism. IBM does not tolerate such behavior!" She went on to say, "I know it must have been difficult, being new, young, and black to endure such pain. However, you must always be strong and demand the respect you deserve. I want you to know that the Regional Director supported Dan's position, believing that it is more important to adhere to IBM principles and policies than to lose a big account with a racist law firm." I said, "This must have been a big decision to let a big law firm account be dropped." She looked at me sternly, "We do not compromise our values. As long as I sit in my role as Regional Support Manager, I will never cave in when it comes to injustice over keeping a client." I felt such respect for her having such strong convictions. She said, "My journey has not been easy; yours will not be either, but what's important is that you work hard, never give up, and stand up for what's right. I predict a great future for you at IBM I will be here for you whenever you need me." She handed me her business card and wrote her personal phone number on the back. She stood up and gave me a big hug just before she left the restaurant. I went back into the restaurant bathroom and broke down and cried.

When I went back to the office, I became a little nervous, not knowing how the Branch Manager would treat me after the decision was made to drop the law firm account, rather than send another person to train the attorney's secretary. I was correct in my feelings; the Branch Manager avoided me like the plague, coming into the training room and directing all his questions at Judy, avoiding all direct contact with me. In addition, for the rest of the week, most of the training I was assigned to do was in the office rather than in the field. Actually, I liked training customers in our office. It was a much more intimate environment and customers enjoyed meeting secretaries from other firms. I worked extraordinarily hard to make the salesmen feel comfortable working with me. I also, remembering Cynthia's encouragement, worked like a beaver to make sure I did an exemplary job, with no missteps. I knew that being black, there was no room for error on my part. I placed undue, but necessary stress, on myself to make everyone like me, smiling cheerfully, and speaking kindly to everyone when I came into the office (even on those days when I didn't feel well). Naively, I came to St. Paul, Minnesota, thinking things were different from Des Moines and times were changing, but learned quickly that racism was still profusely widespread. I was careful not to let my guard down. Realizing that even rising to the top, does not erase the stigma of being judged as a black person; Cynthia reminded me about this. I was happy that Cynthia stayed in touch with me, checking in frequently to see how I was doing. On occasions, we met for private drinks and fun conversations. I felt blessed to have her as my mentor; I believe that she also saw in me someone with whom she could trust and confide in.

IBM opened a larger new office in Minneapolis. I requested a transfer. My transfer was accepted. I was happy to work in Minneapolis, which seemed much more cosmopolitan. There were a lot more salesmen and a few more Educational Service Representatives, who were young and single. The entire working environment seemed more cheerful yet professional. I accompanied many of the salesmen on calls and became more relaxed about going out of the office to train customers. The feedback I received was always positive, which made me more and more confident. I prided myself on dressing professional and always being well prepared. I became more at ease with the salesmen and was invited to join them after work for drinks; I usually made an excuse that I had another engagement. One of the other ESRs, Donna, and I became good friends. I would drag her along with me on the few occasions I joined the guys, not wanting any undue gossip about me going alone.

I was pleasantly surprised when I received a call from Dan, the salesman from the St. Paul office. He said that he was calling to inquire about how I liked the new office and told me that my "buddies," the ones I had gotten to know, missed me and wanted me to join them for a drink. He said Judy would be coming also. I was still moved by the way Dan stood up to the Branch Manager and showed respect and compassion toward me; I thought it would be a nice gesture to accept the invitation. Admittedly, I wasn't too thrilled to go back to the Irish bar in St. Paul, but thought it was important to do so, mainly to show that I wasn't bruised by the law firm incident. It seemed that everyone was happy to see me when I showed up. As it got toward dinnertime everyone, except Dan, said they had to get home to their families. Just as I was going to leave with the group, Dan said, "Why don't you stay and have another drink with me." I agreed. Afterwards, we had dinner together. When he dropped me off, he said, "Let's do it again sometime." After a week, I didn't hear from him so decided that he asked me out as a nice "make-up gesture." The following week, there was a combined meeting with the Minneapolis and St. Paul offices. I saw Dan at the meeting and thought I would walk over to thank him for the dinner, but he continued talking to another sales representative, giving me a slight nod of his head. His reaction, which seemed as a dismissal, infuriated me. Immediately, I thought this was a "white slight" and he didn't want to acknowledge to anyone that we had been out. My first thought went back to my hurtful college experience with Bill, a guy I really cared about. With Dan, it wasn't as though I was dying for him to date me. I just thought he was a nice guy who I would enjoy having dinner or a drink with on occasion. I was hoping that this was the last time I would ever have to see him. I was enjoying being single and dating other guys. I was in a good place during this time of my life. I just didn't like feeling being dismissed and disrespected. I had moved from the "Y," lived in my own apartment, bought a used car, and was making a decent salary, which made it possible for me to send Mama a small check every month. She didn't expect the money; it just made me feel good that I was able to do so. I had reached the pinnacle of being a career woman.

Out of nowhere, I received a call from Dan, as though we had seamlessly kept in touch after we had dinner together. I wasn't overly friendly, but not cold either. We were not in a relationship so I didn't feel I had the right to challenge him for not calling me or saying anything to me when I saw him at the last IBM meeting. He asked if I would like to go to dinner, I said, "I am so sorry but I am busy." I hated these games, but was not going to enthusiastically accept. The third time he called, I broke down and told him I would have dinner with him. After a few drinks, surprising myself, I lit into him and told him I did not appreciate how he ignored me when I saw him at the meeting. I accused him of being uncomfortable by not acknowledging me in front of others because I was black. He was completely dumbstruck upon hearing this rage come from me. I knew immediately that I had gone too far, but didn't know how to dig myself out of the hole I had put myself in. I suggested that we just call it a night and not order dinner. He said, "I think we need to talk about how you are feeling." He proceeded to tell me that he wasn't sure that I would want to go out with him. He had been divorced for two years and said he didn't know how to reenter the dating scene. He told me that it took a lot of courage for him to ask me out because he was afraid that I might reject him. After he shared this confession with me, I felt terrible for the accusations that I spilled on him. I was also angry with myself for making it racial. However, I wanted to protect myself from the melodrama of dating a white guy, and all the ramifications of racism that it may bring with it. I especially did not need the extra baggage of one who was divorced and had a child. I even avoided dating black guys who had been married and had children. I kept thinking we would just remain friends; however, it became a much more serious relationship, neither one of us knowing where it would lead.

My Passion Returns

I cherished working for a company that was as prestigious as IBM. However, I missed teaching and decided to return to the classroom. I applied for a teaching position at Minneapolis Public School District. I was hired to teach high school English at Roosevelt High School. The majority of my students were white. For many of my students, I was their first black teacher. I was one of few black teachers who taught at the high school. The students reminded me of the students where I did my student teaching at Yankton High School. They seemed to appreciate having a teacher who looked different than they, and the few minorities seemed to look up to me as someone whom they could identify. The students were all very respectful and eager to learn. The faculty and administrators were kind and friendly. I seemed to have found my perfect niche. One of the first teachers I met, Carolyn, who was a few years younger than I, became my best friend. We both came from ethnic backgrounds that were diverse, Carolyn being Jewish and I being black. Carolyn taught English in the room next to mine. She was tiny, cute, and petite. She had an amiable spirit and was very witty. Unlike me, who laughed loud and exuberantly when I thought something was funny. Carolyn laughed soft and gentle. We both shared our deep love for teaching and had great relationships with our students. I received two great compliments from two of my former students who were in my English class. One stated that she became an English teacher because of my influence and the other was from a former student named David, who contacted me after 40 years, telling me that he never forgot how kind I was to him. He came from a dysfunctional family. He told me that I always took time to listen to him. Both of these compliments reminded me of why I loved teaching so much. Teaching at Roosevelt High School was a wonderful experience. I was honored by the compliments. My anxiety attacks had all but disappeared.

Carolyn and I enjoyed sharing one another's culture. I enjoyed Carolyn's brisket and Matzo Ball soup, traditional dishes that were served during Yom Kippur, one of the most religious Jewish holidays; and, Carolyn enjoyed my black-eyed peas and collard greens, which was a traditional dish that most black people served on New Year's. When Carolyn decided that she was ready to move from her parents' home, I suggested that we become roommates. We became more like sisters and got along very well. Carolyn became friends with an IBM colleague of Dan's, who was black. The two of them really enjoyed each other's company. Both were extremely intelligent. Dan and I began to date more frequently, establishing a much more serious relationship. Both Carolyn and I were amused that we were both dating guys who were of different ethnicities than the two of us. Dan moved in an apartment complex that was close to where Carolyn and I lived. He became friends with Archie, a former NFL football player. Archie was really fun and had great parties, which Carolyn and I enjoyed. Archie and Dan became great buddies. Before Archie, Dan had never had a close black male friend. In fact, I believe Archie was his first genuine black friend. They fished and hunted together. Archie taught Dan how to make New Orleans's Gumbo, which Dan made for every Super Bowl game. I introduced Archie to Shirley, who became his girlfriend. My hometown girlfriends and I began to see each other more often. We all became a great group of friends who socialized together. I liked the feeling of being surrounded with a diverse group of friends with whom I could be myself: fully at ease with my blackness, laughing loudly and using gestures that black people use as they express themselves. Carolyn continued to be tickled at how I was able to transition by acting totally black when my hometown friends came to visit. I began to realize that since leaving my hometown, most of my interactions evolved around being with white friends and colleagues. It had become almost natural for me to assimilate into a white culture. I had been programmed to know how to "act white" around white people ever since I was a little girl. I appreciated having friends of an array of ethnicities and cultures.

After dating Dan for three years, he and I decided to get married. Dan had trepidations in the beginning, not because I was black but because he had gone through a divorce, and was afraid to make a commitment. I circled a date on the calendar and told him that if he was not ready to make a decision by that date, we would remain friends, but I would start dating other men. Needless to say, he quickly agreed to the date that I circled on the calendar and we started planning our wedding. We had a beautiful intimate wedding at Fort Knox Chapel in St. Paul, Minnesota. Lois, another friend, from Iowa, was my bridesmaid. We bought our matching dresses at a sidewalk sale. Dave, a friend of mine who lived next door to me in our apartment complex, was Dan's best man. Friends from both of our apartment buildings attended our wedding. After our wedding, our friends joined us at Dave's apartment for champagne and dessert. It was a very informal and intimate, but extraordinary wedding. Dan and I went to Las Vegas for our honeymoon. It seemed surreal to be called Mr. & Mrs. Kinney when we checked into the hotel.

Dan and my wedding

It was so interesting that white acquaintances would inquire about how Dan's family felt about Dan marrying someone black, never a question about how my family would feel. Dan's mother, with whom I became very close, inquired,

"What about when you have children?" These questions seemed to be the common "concerns" that white people would ask. My response was, "Our kids will be just fine if people don't see them as being different!" I don't recall a black person ever asking me this question.

Dan and I enjoyed living in Minneapolis. Neither of us wanted to have children right away, giving ourselves time to get to know each other as a married couple. Lisa, Dan's three-year-old daughter, spent every other weekend with Dan and me. My apartment girlfriends and I took Lisa shopping and to Saturday matinees. Dan and I travelled out of the country during my Spring Break and we partied with our friends on weekends. It was like being a "single" married couple. Our carefree lifestyle did not change that much after we got married. We continued to stay connected with our circle of friends, most of whom were still single. Little did we know that our freewheeling life style was about to reshape us as a married couple. We would no longer have our close-knit friends to rely on as our fun-loving support system.

Striking Out on Our Own

The second year into our marriage, Dan was transferred to Milwaukee, Wisconsin. Although it was a lucrative promotion, we both knew that we would desperately miss our friends, with whom we had become so close. We heard negative reports, from several people, about Milwaukee being a blue-collar city. However, since Dan's goal was to become Branch Manager, this position placed him on the trajectory to move up the ladder with IBM Even though I was really sad that we had to move, I stayed positive for Dan and never complained. One evening, while I was sitting and reading the paper, Dan asked me, "Are you feeling okay about the move? I can always turn down the promotion." I gave him a cheery response, not wanting to look up at him, "No, I am looking forward to a new start," while woefully holding back tears. I didn't tell him that I already missed leaving my students at Roosevelt High School, the same way I felt leaving my students in Des Moines to go work for IBM However, this time it was different. I liked living in Minneapolis and felt a certain security being around my diverse friends, who had become like family to me. We celebrated holidays, birthdays, and dinners together. I loved when we had our dance parties at Archie's, dancing to The Temptations, Donna Summers, Commodores, Al Green, and all the other 60s hit songs. I also was fearful that our marriage would not be secure without the support of the closely-knit friends we had developed in Minneapolis. We were moving where we knew absolutely no one.

We rented an apartment in Brown Deer, a suburb of Milwaukee. The first woman I met, Sandy, introduced herself to me. Sandy was very kind and had a cute German accent. She and I became friends and started playing Scrabble and drank gin giblets while our husbands were at work. She told me that her husband was a racist and would not like it if he knew she was coming to my apartment. However, he eventually warmed up to me when he found out Dan liked to fish. He was a very controlling man. Sandy told me that if he came to bed without wearing his underwear, that meant he wanted to have sex. I found that to be hilarious.

I introduced myself to our other neighbor, Jean, who lived directly across the hall from my apartment. I didn't feel that she would introduce herself to me if I didn't make the first move. I saw her several times when we were at the mailbox, but she would get her mail without looking at me and hurriedly would rush back to her apartment. One sunny day while I was sitting on the steps outside of our apartment, Jean came outside with her darling little blond-haired boy and sat down beside me. She started interrogating me as though she was an F.B.I. agent, asking me several questions about Dan and me. The shocker was when she said that she heard that Dan and I "lived together" and weren't really married. I was so insulted that I went to my apartment to get our wedding certificate. I showed it to her as proof. I was so angry with myself for doing so. I asked myself, "Why did you have to prove to her that you were married? You didn't have to prove anything to her." I had very little to do with her after that. I thought about when President Obama was pressured to present his birth certificate to prove and appease ignorant and racist people, that he was an American citizen. Jean's husband never spoke to me so I knew that he was in the same "camp" with Sandy's husband. On occasion, he would speak to Dan; however, Dan wanted to have nothing to do with him.

Eventually, we moved to a nice, newly built house in another suburb, called Bayside. The families in our neighborhood were very nice; all were college graduates and professionals in their fields, twenty notches more sophisticated than the people in the apartments where we lived. I was bored and ready to return to teaching.

I applied for a teaching position in the Milwaukee Public School District. I was called in for an interview almost within a week's time of sending in my application. I was offered a position to teach high school English at one of the largest inner-city high schools, a school where most of the teachers and students were minority. I was overjoyed to be placed at a school where I would be teaching minority students. I also thought it would be great to teach with other minority teachers who were committed to teaching inner-city students. The year was 1974; feelings among many blacks toward whites were still relatively raw. I received a few "rolled eyes" from, blacks when Dan and I were at the grocery store or at a shopping mall. The looks were directed at me. I don't believe Dan noticed, or if he did, he never told me. I didn't want to make him aware for fear it might cause an unnecessary problem. Dan was not afraid of standing up to anyone, if he believed the person was trying to be intimidating or was being disrespectful. I learned this about him when he dealt with the law firm situation at IBM in St. Paul.

What I didn't expect was the treatment I received the first day I arrived at the high school. It was apparent by the "cold" treatment I received from some of the black teachers, which felt like a "Not Welcome" sign. I have always been one to try and make people feel comfortable around me, by smiling, giving compliments, or trying to make small talk, believing people will feel differently if they get to know me as a person. I was used to being the one who made this first move, with racist white people, not blacks. I tried many times to talk to several teachers in the faculty lounge, but would receive short answers, while they continued their conversations with other teachers. After a few weeks, I was completely blindsided by hateful racist notes placed in my teacher's mailbox, as well as under my car windshield wiper. Notes written such as, "Black during the day and white at night." I questioned whether I should report these messages to the principal, but fearful things might get worse, I choose not to. My refuge was in the classroom. The students were very kind and I enjoyed teaching my classes. I believe the students could sense the tension and felt sorry that the other black teachers were not kind to me. When I arrived home in the evening, I was stressed, sad, and lonely. I dreaded going to school every day and almost ran to my classroom as soon as I arrived. I kept this cruelty to myself; I didn't want to share it with anyone, not even Dan. I eventually told Dan what I was experiencing at school. He was furious and angry at me for not telling him sooner. He wanted to go to the school and confront the principal and even suggested that we get law enforcement involved. I convinced him to see if things got better. In retrospect, I probably should have reported the racist remarks left on my car; it certainly was no different if the notes were from white supremacists. Blacks should not have received a "pass." The treatment I received at this high school was more hurtful to me than the racism I experienced by the racist attorney at the law firm. Sadly, I believe I was too afraid to do anything about what was happening to me. These were my own people, yet I feared them.

Several months into the second school year, I learned that I was pregnant with our first child. My immediate concern was how our child was going to be treated when she started school if we continued to live in Milwaukee. I had already begun investigating private schools before the baby was even born. Erica, our first child, was born in the summer, which gave me time to be on maternity leave until after Thanksgiving, and more time to spend with Erica. More importantly, it gave me a reprieve from the ugliness I was experiencing at school. Dan tried to convince me to resign; I was determined not to allow the mean-spirited teachers to think they were the reason for my not returning. When it was time to return to school, I planned to report to law enforcement and the administrators the evidence of the racial notes, which I had kept and dated. I was returning with a vengeance. I was not going to allow these bullies to intimidate me any longer. Dan was promoted to a new position in Detroit, Michigan, before my maternity leave was up. I had been rescued from this toxic environment.

I was adversely affected, really more shell-shocked, by my horrific experience while teaching in Milwaukee. When we moved, I decided to stay home and be mom. A couple of months went by when I unexpectedly received a call from IBM, inquiring if I was interested in coming back to work part-time. It was a perfect offer. I would have an opportunity to stay at home with Erica and still do something I enjoyed. My new neighbor, Sandy, was a full-time stay-at-home mom; she agreed to babysit Erica. Sandy had three darling kids and a wonderful husband. Everyone in the family spoiled Erica.

I loved working at the IBM Detroit office. Dan worked in the same building on a different floor. We seldom saw each other, but thought it important that we keep our business and personal lives separate. I became friends with a woman named Jamie. Jamie was almost 6 feet tall and had a big Afro. She had a great sense of humor and was always smiling. She was one of the most seasoned and most competent E.S.R.s in the Detroit office. Everyone admired her. All the sales representatives vied for Jamie to accompany them on customer calls. Jamie did not have children. She loved coming to our house to see Erica. She bought Erica her first black doll. In the 70s, the doll companies were attempting to manufacture dolls that showed diversity; the white dolls had blonde silky hair and blue eyes, like the one I received when I was a child, whereas, the black dolls had very dark skin with kinky black hair and black eyes. Erica named her doll Jamie. She carried her doll with her at all times, including to bed. Erica wanted to give her doll, Jamie, a bath. She washed her hair with her baby shampoo. Poor Jamie's body was made of cloth and her hair came out like an S.O.S. pad. Erica cried when Jamie's body became waterlogged and her hair became stiff and hard. I tried drying Jamie out and put her in the dryer. Jamie never looked the same again, but Erica still carried her around everywhere and slept with her every night.

We lived in a very friendly suburb, called Farmington Hills. The neighbors embraced our family from the first day we moved in. The neighborhood kids knocked on our door almost every day after school, asking if they could take Erica for a walk in the stroller. Erica especially loved Michelle, Sandy's oldest daughter, who was in middle school. Michelle, like her mother, was a pretty little girl with a happy smile. Erica called her "Shelley." She always wanted to brush Shelley's hair and Shelley let her do it. Michelle became a great help to me. While she played with Erica, I was able to fix dinner and do a few chores around the house. I offered to pay her for helping me; however, her mother said it was good experience for Michelle to help and preferred that I not pay her. I made sure I had special treats for the kids when they came over after school, and picked up little girlie things for Michelle. When Erica had her one-year birthday party, almost every child and adult in the neighborhood attended. We were the only biracial couple who lived in the neighborhood; however, the other neighbors all came from culturally diverse backgrounds. We all shared our ethnic cuisines. My neighbor, Madeline, was Armenian. She made the best eggplant dish I had ever tasted. She and I also took belly dance lessons together, which she told me was a traditional Armenian dance. I never was good at learning the moves; I decided to quit the belly dance class and enrolled in a Jazzercise class. Tony and Charlene, who were also friendly neighbors, lived across the street from us. Tony was Italian and known for his mouth-watering spicy dishes. Our other neighbor, Marilyn, was Jewish who invited the entire neighborhood to join her family to celebrate Seder, a ceremonial diner to mark the beginning of Pass-over. My friend Carolyn had already introduced me to brisket and Matzo Ball soup, which Marilyn made scrumptiously as well. I was known for my collard greens and bourbon yams, which I served during Thanksgiving.

Living in Farmington Hills was like living in an international village, and just minutes away from downtown Detroit. Farmington Hills was a wonderful relief from the drama I experienced while living in Milwaukee. Dan and I frequently went into the city to eat, shop and attend events. Ironically, before we moved to Detroit, both black and white acquaintances "warned" us about all the danger and racism we would face while living in Detroit. We found it to be one of most diverse and friendliest cities, where we could have lived.

Lake No Negro

Just as we were feeling that Farmington Hills was going to be the place that we would settle down and raise our family, Dan received another promotion. This time our move would be to Portland, Oregon. Although we regretted leaving our friends, there was a certain excitement moving to a place where neither of us had ever visited. Erica was especially sad that she wouldn't see "Shelley." She asked about her for a long time after we moved. We had heard from several people how beautiful Portland was. My mother told me that she heard that Portland was referred to as "God's Country." When we arrived to meet our realtor, it was a beautiful day, aesthetically green, with beautiful pine trees surrounding the city. What we failed to know was that it rained approximately 142 days a year, without sun. The day we visited happened to be one out of the 142 days that it wasn't raining. The bright sun shining on Mt. Hood made the mountain appear as a beautiful diamond in the sky.

Dan made several calls to IBM colleagues who were working in Portland to inquire about best locations to live. His contacts, as well as the realtor, told us that Lake Oswego was the most upscale suburb to live and was known to have one of the best school districts in the state of Oregon. After hearing raving comments and researching the area more on our own, we decided to purchase a home in Lake Oswego. The realtor showed us a home in Mountain Park, a subdivision of Lake Oswego. It was a thriving new area where families with young children were moving. The homes also were more reasonably priced than the homes around the lake. To our happiness, we found a home that Dan and I both liked. We were especially fortunate to learn that our next-door neighbor had a young daughter the same age as Erica. A few days after we moved in, I took Erica next door to introduce ourselves. The husband, looking somewhat annoyed, reluctantly opened the door. I introduced Erica and myself, stammering uncomfortably, to share that we were the new neighbors and understood that he and his wife had a daughter Erica's age. I continued to say, "I thought it might be fun for them to meet." Leaving the door partially open, he walked away and yelled to his wife. "There's someone at the door." I was somewhat uneasy, not knowing what to expect when his wife came to the door. The wife arrived, looking nervous, but was smiling and had a pleasant look on her face. Her two daughters came to the door behind her, wanting to see who their mother was speaking to. The mother stepped outside, gently pushing her two girls in front of her and closed the door. She was a pretty woman with freckles, who looked much younger than her husband. She had her long caramel-colored hair pulled back into a ponytail. Kami, the three-year-old daughter, and Erica connected immediately, both giggling and chasing each other around the front yard in a circle. Dana, the mother (pseudonym), said, "Thank you for coming by. I think it would be fun to get the girls together. Give me your phone number and I will call you." She did not give me her phone number. The very next day, Dana called to ask if Kami could come to our house to play. I was delighted, knowing how much Erica missed her friends in Detroit. I was a little puzzled that she didn't invite Erica to play at her house, since Erica was the new kid; however, I actually felt more comfortable having the girls play at our house, especially not knowing anything about Kami's family. Dana and I were neighborly but did not become social friends. Her husband remained very distant, only speaking if I spoke to him first. After I told Dan about the "chilly" reception I received from Dana's husband, he made it clear, "I don't care if we ever get together with the two of them." He was very protected of Erica and me, if he sensed there were racial overtones.

One day when I invited Dana over for tea, I knew something was strange when she said she would come over after her husband left for work. When she came over, she sadly shared with me that her husband was very controlling. She said that she was not even allowed to read a book when he was home because he wanted all of her attention. He wouldn't allow her to drive downtown

Portland; he told her it was too dangerous, which it definitely was not. She seemed to be in an emotionally abusive marriage. I did not give her my opinion about what I thought about her husband; I didn't feel it was any of my business. I felt sorry for her. It surprised me that her husband didn't seem to mind that Erica and Kami played together. Dan and I met two other neighbors, who lived down the street. Each of the neighbors came to introduce themselves and their children. Nanette, the first neighbor to come, welcomed our family warmly, bringing homemade dessert and a toy for Erica. She was excited that Jennifer, her daughter, had a new friend to play with. She, without hesitation, invited Erica to her house to play with Jennifer. Nanette's husband, Larry, and Dan became instant friends. They both joined Indian Princesses together, a dad-and-daughter organization. After meeting Nanette, I met another wonderful and friendly woman named Pat, while she was strolling her daughter, Brooke, past our house. Pat and I became immediate friends, finding out that we both lived in Detroit before moving to Lake Oswego. Before long, Ali was born and four of the little girls became close friends and, all played together almost daily. Dan and I socialized with both families. We didn't make an effort to socialize with the couple that lived next door, hearing that they also didn't socialize with any of the other neighbors. Being the only black person who lived in our neighborhood, I seemed to constantly have my "feelers" out. I didn't like allowing my suspiciousness to make me presume that a white person must be racist if they did not instantly take to me. I was truly working on not being so self-absorbed by "reading into" what I thought others were thinking.

I found that many of the women who lived around the more exclusive area of Lake Oswego were stay-at-home moms, who relished that their husbands were CEOs or in other high-paying professional positions. BMWs and Mercedes lined the grocery store lot. One of the ladies, who was aware that Dan was the Branch Manager of IBM, reached out to me and invited me to be a guest at a Lake Oswego Women's Club. I had never been a big fan of joining any women's club, not even the black sororities that I was invited to pledge. After growing up with so many sisters, I preferred men friends rather than being around a group of women. However, since I was new in the community, I thought attending the women's club might give Dan and me an opportunity to meet other couples. Jan (pseudonym) picked me up and drove me to be her guest at the meeting. She explained to me, "Members are permitted to bring guests to assess whether the club is a good fit for the club, as well as for the members. However, we rarely bring new people to our meetings." I thought it was kind that she included me to such an exclusive group of women. Jan didn't tell me what the criteria were to determine how it was decided if the guest was a good fit or not. The meeting began with introductions, by giving our name and telling what our husband's occupation was. There did not seem to be any interest in knowing how many children one had, what the woman's interest was, or what, if any, professional field one may be in. The first woman, Emily (pseudonym), began by saying, "Hi. My name is Emily and my husband makes lots of money!" I thought this was a joke and laughed slightly. Then I realized she was serious. I found out that her husband owned a big financial firm. When it was my turn to speak, I said, "My name is Paula and my husband, Dan, babysits Erica and Ali and also takes out the trash." I could see by the looks on the women's shocked faces that they weren't sure what to say, or knew if I was being serious. I kept a straight face, to keep them guessing. I knew I was being sarcastic, and regretted afterwards that I was being so flippant. I already felt uncomfortable being the only black person in the room. Besides, I did not feel comfortable with this group of women nor fit in with them; they seemed to behave with such entitlement. It was difficult to wear my "happy mask." I don't know how I passed the litmus test; however, Jan called to tell me that I was accepted into the club. She shared with me that the women said, "Paula is so funny. She doesn't even seem black." Not seeming "black" became a very occurring, much-too-frequent comment from many white people, even from those whom I considered to be my white friends. It took me a long time to respond, "Being black is not a bad thing. I am proud that I am black." I knew that the women's club was not a social group I would want to join. I told Jan that I had too much on my plate and thanked her for the invitation.

Erica and Jennifer started kindergarten together at the local school. Dan and I both had tears in our eyes when Erica, on her very first day of school, stepped aboard the big yellow bus. We wanted Erica to have the experience of riding on the bus. I drove to the school so I could meet Erica when she arrived; I wanted also to meet her teacher and see her classroom. It wasn't until I walked into the school with Erica that I realized how little diversity there was—absolutely no diversity in administration, faculty, or staff. I was greeted with lukewarm hellos from the other moms, who were mingling in the hall. I started feeling out of place, but wanted the other moms to know how nice I was by putting on my "I am really a nice person" big smile, pretending that I had it all together. I tried joining in on conversations with some of the moms, but they seemed engaged talking to each other, so I quit. I worked at making white people comfortable around me. I would have been much more comfortable if my neighbor Nanette would have been able to come with me. I became upset with myself for allowing this insecurity to come over me. I quickly peeked in at Erica, who was now sitting at her desk. I threw her a kiss and waved goodbye. I nervously walked briskly to my car.

When Erica returned home from school, she told me about another little girl she played with that looked just like her. During "Back to School Night," I asked Erica to show her dad and me the little girl she played with who looked like her. She pointed to a little girl standing not far from us. Her name was Tianna and she was a cute little Korean girl who was adopted from Korea. Erica already attached herself to a little girl who looked "different" from the other kids. Tianna's mother, who was white, was pleasantly amused when I told her how Erica told her dad and me that Tianna looked like Erica.

By the time Erica reached fourth grade, I was beginning to notice that she was showing minor signs of withdrawal; she seldom smiled. She no longer seemed to be very happy at school and began not wanting to go to school at all. I finally was able to get her to open up to me why she did not like school. She told me some boys at school teased her every day and continually called her "chocolate milk face." I was heartbroken to hear that she had been suffering this hurt, by herself, without saying anything. I remembered back how I felt when I was a little girl and was called an unkind name. The difference was, Erica did not have me with her to comfort her as I did, having my mother with me. I addressed the bullying that Erica was experiencing to the principal. He smiled, which irritated me, and said, "This is just playful joking. The boys don't mean anything by it. They are just being boys." Whoa! I wanted to seriously slap him. I became fully aware how culturally ignorant he was. I explained to the principal that besides being bullied, the boys were making racial remarks toward my daughter. I told him that it made me very upset that he didn't understand how a child of color feels being called names that referred to the color of her skin and was teased daily by students, without any support from an adult. I inquired, "Why were no adults around on the playground to stop the harassment?" His response was, "They are on the playground however they don't discipline kids who are just having fun." He continued, "Besides,

Erica didn't say anything to the teachers on the playground. We always tell our students to go to an adult if a student is being picked on by another student." I was so frustrated. The principal really didn't "get it." He truly lacked cultural proficiency. Seeing how upset I was becoming, he said, "I will talk to the boys." I could tell by his response that the "talk" was not going to be a serious talk. I was feeling so conflicted, asking myself several questions, *Should I take Erica out of the school this very moment? Did we do the right thing by moving into such a white conservative suburb, where there's truly white privilege and entitlement? Would it had been better if we moved to North East Portland, where there was much more diversity, rather than Lake Oswego, which was lily white?*

Dan and I discussed the possibility of taking Erica out of school and placing her in a private school that was more diverse. Erica was very adamant about not leaving her school and her friends. We were torn, however, and believed we would be making a mistake if we took her out of school where she had made a few close friends. She was at a very pivotal age. However, I was beginning to observe that Erica's self-esteem was beginning to be affected. She was becoming more aware of her biracial culture and ashamed of her brown skin. She wanted to look and be like her white friends. Although she had soft brown curly hair, not kinky, she wanted her hair to be straight. I started taking her to the same beauty parlor where I went to get my hair straightened, using the same process: applying harsh lye to her hair, which usually left the scalp burning and the hair dry. She was so proud to bounce her straight hair around. This was déjà vu, a repeat of what I experienced as a child.

Erica even appeared embarrassed when I came to her school; I believe it was because I had dark skin, not white like the other kids' mothers. She would say things to me like, "Mom, why do you have to talk so loud?" I could feel her stiffening as I walked up to hug her when she got off the bus from a field trip. It was not the normal embarrassing way that most kids her age reacted if their parents hugged them in front of friends; her reaction was more of a repulsive response. I ached for her. I reflected back on my own feelings of insecurity. My feelings of embarrassment were because of my mother's light skin.

After my conversation with the principal, it was obvious to me, by the administration and faculty's guarded and fake friendliness toward me when I came to school that I was viewed as the abrasive, angry black parent. I was really troubled when it was time to enroll Ali, our youngest daughter, in the same school. Ali was such a happy child, always smiling and very outgoing.

She was in commercials before she was four and, at the age of five, was one of the children's news anchors on a major children's program called *Popcorn*, never forgetting any of her lines. She became an accomplished young actor who was very confident. I began to worry that her confidence and self-esteem could be damaged if she experienced the same difficulties that Erica endured while at school.

By second grade, I began to notice some of the "hidden" unhappy symptoms in Ali that Erica exhibited. Ali seemed a little more anxious and bothered by something that I couldn't put my finger on. When I asked her about school, she would always say, "Everything is okay." When I probed more about her friendships, her reply was, "I like all of my friends." Ali continued to work at, outwardly, displaying her cheerful disposition, not wanting to let anyone know if she was sad or hurt. She took after me in this regard.

One day when Ali got off the bus, I noticed a little paper-shaped orange paper turtle pinned to Ali's sweater. At first I thought it was artwork that Ali made at school. However, when I inquired about it, she embarrassingly told me that it was placed on the "slow" kids who did not finish their math quizzes on time. I asked her if this was the first time she had a turtle pinned on her and she said, "No, I took the others off before I got off the bus." I was so infuriated that I could hardly breathe, but did not want Ali to see my anger so I gently removed the turtle from her sweater. I knew it was imperative for me to go to the school to find out why Ali was having problems in math. Before Dan could put his briefcase down, I told him we were making an appointment to speak with Ali's teacher. I left messages for Ali's teacher, two consecutive days, with no return call. When she finally called, she said, "I am so sorry but I have back-to-back appointments and will not have time to meet with you and your husband after school." I responded curtly, "My husband and I will meet with you during the day, before school, or during your planning period." Dan and I were willing to rearrange our schedules to meet with her at any time. This was very urgent to us. She reluctantly agreed to meet us a week later and informed us that she would like the principal to be present in the meeting with us. My husband and I waited for 20 minutes before the teacher and principal said they were ready to meet with us. My inclination told me the two of them were deciding how to respond to the angry black woman and her husband.

The conference began with the teacher chitchatting, "So how are things going? Are you pretty settled in with your new move? I really like having Ali in my class. This has been a good start of the school year." I promised myself that I would be courteous and patiently let her continue with annoying, small nosy chatter. What I really wanted to say was, "Cut the bullshit and let's discuss Ali!" Her gibber was really getting on my nerves. I especially didn't like the artificial smile and the demeaning way she continued her conversation as though Dan and I were clueless nitwits. The principal sat quietly with his arms crossed and was expressionless. I finally stated firmly to the teacher, "Dan needs to get back to work and I have errands to run. It's important that we begin our discussion regarding Ali's math progress." I went on to say, as my eyes looked directly at the principal, "We have already lost 20 minutes of our appointment time while the two of you were in your own private meeting." Dan looked at me as though to say, "Cool it." Taking Dan's cue, I politely changed my stance, "We would like to see Ali's math assignments." The teacher said, "Before I go over her assignments, I would like to tell you that Lake Oswego is very committed to making sure that all of our students meet learning goals by meeting specific clock time while testing." I was becoming very annoyed. I could feel the tension building up in Dan, his calmness dissipating. He reiterated my request forcefully, "We would like to review Ali's math work!" Dan and I fastidiously looked over all of Ali's assignments. We arrived at the same conclusion almost simultaneously. All of Ali's math problems were correct, although she had not completed all the problems on some of her work sheets. The teacher smiled smugly, "As you can see, Ali is *not capable* of finishing her work when the buzzer goes off." I was fuming, but was able to maintain my composure. Dan was not as composed, "Are you telling me that it is more important for a student to finish all the work by the time a ridiculous buzzer goes off rather than assessing her understanding of the math concepts?" The teacher replied back, arrogantly, "At Lake Oswego, we are preparing our students for college. Timed tests are required, even as early as kindergarten. Lake Oswego School District gets superb state academic ratings." She continued, "It is apparent Ali is unable to keep up." I looked at my husband and said, "Obviously, this is not the right school for Ali." I stood up and replied, "We also have high expectations for our daughters to attend college. It's apparent you don't have the same expectations for Ali." I continued, "We will be withdrawing Ali from school at the end of *this* school day!" As we walked out of the building, Dan looked at me and said, "Hon, that was a little drastic. I agree with you for being so upset about Ali, just as I am; however, you and I didn't even have an opportunity to discuss next steps, nor have we had the time to forewarn Ali that she will be changing schools." He continued, "We don't even know where Ali will be attending her next school." I knew that I had acted abruptly and too impulsive. My fury of emotions had got the best of me; nevertheless, I wasn't going to allow our daughter to be demeaned and embarrassed by having a turtle pinned on her clothes. I had observed minority kids in the schools where I taught being devalued by teachers. I had been one of those kids. It was difficult for Dan to feel the full impact of how degrading it feels for a minority student to be belittled in front of their peers. It is wrong for any student to endure this kind of embarrassment; for a minority student, it feels painfully hurtful.

I drove home, with tears flowing down my face. Ali was unaware of the teacher's wrenching remarks, yet I believe Ali knew that she was treated differently than the other children. I felt as though I had been punched in the gut. I repeatedly heard the teacher's words. *"Not capable."* I screamed out in my car, "Bitch, you are going to eat your words!" I had heard about a prestigious progressive private school named The Catlin Gable School, which had an exemplary reputation for challenging students academically, while focusing on their individual learning style. The school emerged in my mind as the perfect school for Ali. I knew one of the professional basketball players' wives whose children were attending this school. She was an active volunteer at Catlin. I called her and she graciously offered to see if she could set up an appointment for me to meet the Head Master. He and I had a wonderful discussion about the school culture, the curricula, and the staff. I received a call later that afternoon from the Admission's Director inviting Ali to "shadow" another student the very next day.

At the end of the school day, as I walked toward Ali, she was beaming. She looked euphoric. The teacher hugged her and the other children were smiling and saying goodbye. That evening, I received a phone call from the Headmaster, Mr. Scott, informing me that Ali could start school on Monday. I was flabbergasted! He said, "We will still need to receive the records from Lake Oswego, but we don't perceive there will be any problems." I believe He knew how desperate we were to find a new school. It was very unusual for Catlin to accept students without going through the full interview process. Mr. Scott said, "Ali appears to be a perfect fit. She is a very sweet and intelligent little girl. She was immediately liked by both her teachers and the students." Ali told her dad and me, "Some of the students told me that they saw me on *Popcorn*." Ali told us that she was embarrassed so she told them, "That was a girl who looks like me." She said later she told them the truth. Her dad and I thought that was hilarious. Ali loved Catlin Gable School. Ali flourished and did extremely well academically and not, surprisingly, socially.

I was not aware that Ali's records from Lake Oswego Elementary School arrived at Catlin two weeks after Ali was already attending school. The Admissions Director revealed that she had called the school several times to request them. I was not surprised that the school did not make sending the records a priority. I was not told until Ali had been attending the school, three years later, that when the records finally arrived, the Catlin Admissions Director thought the records must have been for another student. The records disclosed that, "Ali would **not** be a good candidate for Catlin Gable because she is academically delayed and had been recommended for Special Education." I was furious! I shrieked, "Why were we not told about the contents of these records?" The Headmaster replied, "Ali had already proven she was a strong academic student, and I believed that it would have been too hurtful for you and Dan to learn what the records revealed." I was enraged and told Mr. Scott that he had no right to keep this information from us. The Headmaster agreed and said, "In hindsight, it was only right that you should have been shown the records. It's just that Ali was doing so well." He continued to say, " Had Lake Oswego sent the records on time, Catlin Gable would not have had the privilege of having Ali attend the school." This comment softened my anger and made me upset with myself for responding so negatively toward Mr. Scott.

I cringed to think about Ali being recommended for Special Education. I thought about how many other minority kids I knew that were placed in Special Education and how they may have flourished if they were given the opportunity to attend a school like Catlin. My sister, Connie, was in Special Education. She was creatively gifted in so many ways; my parents accepted that the school knew best by placing her in a class, not only with students who struggled academically, but also with students with physical disabilities and mental issues. To make matters worse her teacher suffered from Elephantiasis, a disease that caused her body to swell to massive proportions. I recollect how big her feet were. Although the teacher's health problem was not her fault, the students were embarrassed when they walked down the hall with her. I look back and recall seeing the students, mostly minority, walking in a straight line to the playground, as young "misfits." My heart aches when I think back on how Connie must have felt. Many underrepresented parents, especially parents of color, did not have the knowhow or skillsets to advocate for their students. I shudder to think where Ali would be today if Dan and I had not challenged the teacher who pinned the orange turtle on our young daughter. Ali's future was much brighter. She graduated from NYU, on the Dean's List, and today is an accomplished screenwriter.

Shooting from the Hip

Feeling things were going extremely well with Ali and Erica and both more settled in school, I was feeling unfulfilled not working and longed to be back in the classroom. I mailed in my credentials and applied for a position with Portland Public School District. I was hired to teach at a high school, which wasn't too far from where I lived. I recall being very nervous when I was interviewed, always wanting to make sure I responded to questions with confidence, articulated properly and looked professional. There were always reoccurring questions in the back of my mind whenever I interviewed, *Would my being black be a factor? Am I being hired because I am black, by fulfilling a diversity quota, without recognizing my strong skillsets?*

I recall Dr. Taylor (pseudonym), the principal of the high school, coming out and greeting me with a robust handshake. He was almost the exact replica of whom I imagined Abraham Lincoln would look like. He was a very tall man with a warm smile. He had a pipe cuffed in his hand. He invited me to sit down in the chair in front of his desk, while he sat behind. The entire time during our interview, he puffed on his pipe; I never saw any smoke coming out. My interview lasted almost an hour. I liked Dr. Taylor instinctively.

I knew when I was hired that it was one of the schools where black students would be transported in order to reduce the pattern of residential segregation. Even knowing this, I was disheartened that black students were bussed to the white community, for the purpose of desegregation, rather than having white students bussed to the black community. It was not unusual for black students to be the ones who should assimilate with white students, as a desegregation method. What saddened me was that many black parents supported desegregation bussing, not so much for integration but believing that their students would receive a better education if they attended school with a majority of white students and teachers. Sadly, in some instances this was true. I understood this mentality because this was the way I was raised, to emulate and learn the ways of white people in order to be successful. I grew up becoming proficient at being able to switch personas, one around white people and another around blacks.

In spite of my adverse feelings about the black students being bussed, not to mention knowing the students had to ride a long distance from their community, I was committed to help build relationships among the black and white students. I wanted to be a role model for both. I enjoyed teaching students from both sides of the river, and began to notice more interaction between the two groups of students, especially with the young men who played sports together. I began thinking of ways that I might build a bridge between the students who were bussed to the school and the students who lived in the white community. I requested permission from Dr. Taylor to start a community relations club, which he was pleased for me to do. He said, "I think this will be a great first step for our students to become better acquainted. You have my full support." After meeting with a few interested students, the students formed a club and named it "Hands Across the Bridge." I was so proud of how many students joined and appeared to be making valuable friendships.

During Black History Month, the students produced a moving play, portraying the atrocity of racism and the disparity of social injustice. The students spent hours, during lunch and after school, planning the assembly. Many of the bussed students took public transportation so they could stay after school and work on the play. When it was time for the play to be seen, all classes were dismissed to attend. The students were so excited about their work. To my dismay, I found that few teachers and not any administrators attended the play. I felt disappointed for the students; I believed their neglecting to attend sent a message to the students that the play was not meaningful. After the students returned to class, I met with Dr. Taylor to tell him how disappointed I was that few of the faculty and not any of the administrators attended. He and I had, what I thought, was a good relationship and shared similar philosophical beliefs. He had visited my classes on several occasions and complimented me on my preparation and how well I related to the students. I was unnerved by how our conversation proceeded. I said to him, "Dr. Taylor, this play was a wonderful opportunity for students and faculty to witness the importance of diverse people interacting together. The students were compassionate about the message they were trying to convey." I continued, "This was difficult enough for the bussed students to reveal how they feel being a minority. This play gave them an opportunity to be engaged with the white students in a positive way." I could see that Dr. Taylor could hear from the tone of my voice that I was angry and upset. The smile he usually displayed disappeared. He said to me, "Paula, don't get so upset. This was just a play. I have never seen you shoot from the hip like this before. You are always smiling and so friendly. Now you are coming across as an angry black woman." I could not believe what I was hearing. I knew better than to reply back with a spiteful reply. As I stood in front of him, I could feel my heart palpitating. I felt tears well up, but I was not going to let them flow down my face in front of him. I said submissively, "I thought you would understand." I turned and walked away. Our relationship was never the same again. I felt isolated and alone, knowing that other teachers had heard that I complained about them not attending the assembly. I asked myself the same question that I had asked myself so many times, "Why does this have to be so damn hard?"

Each time I saw the big yellow bus drive up to the school, I wanted to go outside and scream loudly, "Take the students back to their own community, where they will feel wanted." Often the bus was late because of traffic. Students reported to me that one of the teachers, more than once, would say to them as they entered the room with their excused note, which they had to stop by the main office to pick up, making them even later, "So, your bus was late AGAIN!" This embarrassing comment was made in front of the entire class. The teacher would continue to chastise them, "You will have to come during lunch to catch up with the 15 minutes you missed." I was outraged when the students told me about these heartless remarks; however, I held back my feelings in front of them. I would respond back to them warmly, "Make sure you make up the class during lunchtime so you don't fall behind." Even though I felt bad for the students, I did not want them to fall behind in their class and receive bad grades. I wanted the students to do well in spite of how much I identified with their hurt feelings. I did not want to appear to show preferential treatment toward them. I valued my students; the ones who lived in the community and the ones who took the long ride across town. The Community Relations Committee continued to flourish and many students from both sides of the river began to socialize together, after school and on the weekends. This made my three-year teaching position at the high school well worth the time I spent there.

The "School within a School"

I was ecstatic when I was appointed to be vice principal in charge of the performing arts at an urban high school. The community surrounding the school was poor and had a reputation for being unsafe by some who lived outside of the community. In addition, annually the school was reported by the Department of Education as having one of the lowest academic ratings in the district. In spite of the unfavorable reputation, I felt very much at "home." The principal, Mr. Jones, was black and the majority of the administrative team was black. It seemed that all of the faculty and administrators, regardless of race, were committed and dedicated to the school and to each other. Although almost all minorities attended, it was a much different environment than the experience I encountered at the high school in Milwaukee, Wisconsin. There was one caveat; located within the neighborhood high school, was a renowned magnet program. Mr. Jones forewarned me that the teachers who taught the students in the magnet program would be challenging to supervise. He told me that two vice principals prior to my being hired resigned because of how disrespectfully they were treated by the magnet school teachers. Mr. Jones informed me, "I hired you because we need someone strong who can stand up to these hard-to-manage teachers." I wasn't so sure about how strong I could be, but was willing to try my best to build a positive working relationship with the teachers, while still having them have respect toward me as their supervisor. It seemed that, the magnet teachers believed they had their own set of rules and policies and did not need to have a vice principal supervise them. The magnet program was nationally recognized and had an exemplary reputation. The performing arts faculty were extraordinary master teachers, each were specialists in their area of expertise. Many had performed with other well-known professional artists in New York and abroad. It was hard to argue that they did not know how to run the magnet program without supervision. The quandary was that the magnet program was not a private program, which is how the arts faculty preferred to view themselves; they were required to abide by the same policies as the neighborhood school for which they resided and were under the same jurisdiction. After maintaining a stronghold, I was able to convince the magnet school faculty to come to terms with complying with school and district policies. I definitely respected their professionalism and high standards, which they required from the students in their program. The dance program, especially, was deemed to be outstanding. The director of the dance program, Mary, had been at the school for 24 years. She established a very elite touring "Dance Company." When the students performed, auditoriums were always at capacity, including when they performed in Russia.

Two distinct schools emerged, a "school within a school," one school for the socioeconomically poor neighborhood students; and one for the magnet students, who were middle- to upper-middle class and came from, comparatively speaking, wealthy neighborhoods. Unlike being bussed for the purpose of desegregation, these students came to enrich their dance and music skills, many wanting to aspire to be accepted at schools like Juilliard or become professional dancers. The majority of the magnet students came part time. They took all of their required classes at their home schools, believing they would not receive a quality education at the neighborhood school where they were enrolled for the magnet program. Unfortunately, many of the minority neighborhood parents had the same perception as the white parents and transferred their students to other schools. Because of this overriding perspective of the high school of not having a solid academic program, it became a self-fulfilling prophecy. With the small number of students enrolled in higher-level advanced classes, it became difficult for the school to offer advanced-level classes.

All magnet students were required to go through an arduous audition process. Few minority students were in the program. Seeing so few minorities in the magnet program brought back memories of me not having the financial means to take music or dance lessons; however, at this school the magnet program was free, yet few minority students were unable to take advantage of the program because many did not meet the audition requirements. I addressed this concern to the magnet program directors and was told that the neighborhood students would lower the quality of the program, because of their lack of commitment. Hearing this information did not set well with me. The principal supported my recommendation that we require all freshman neighborhood students to take level-one dance classes in order to fulfill their Physical Education credit. By imposing this requirement, all students would be exposed to all forms of dance. Prior to this restriction, African Dance was one of the only dance classes the neighborhood students were able to enroll in, without going through an application process.

My office window faced the outside entrance to the school. I watched daily as the busses dropped off the magnet students. Two visions remain with me: The first is watching the privileged magnet students getting off the bus, carrying their instruments or dance clothes in their duffel bags, jubilantly and enthusiastically entering the dilapidated building, with sparse brown grass, where the halls were gloomily lit. The magnet students were unaffected by the appearance outside or inside the building. They were coming to fulfill a purpose and were excited and prepared to attend their classes. They chose to come to this school; it was not forced upon them. The busses picked them up at the end of the day and dropped them off at the school near their privileged homes. They were entitled. The second vision was: seeing the busload of black students getting off the busses, slowly walking as they entered a beautiful red-brick building with manicured lush green grass. The school had big open spaces and was brightly lit. It had a swimming pool and tennis courts. The students who came from across the river, for the purpose of reducing segregation, had little choice where they would attend school. The mandatory-bussed students came into the school with their heads down, looking embarrassed and dejected. Both sets of students came from two different worlds, serving two separate purposes. I had lived in one of the worlds and learned to navigate in the other.

The neighborhood students were extremely respectful toward the administrators and most of their teachers. I believe their parents instilled in them to be respectful, regardless of how they felt, just as mine had instilled in my sisters and me. Parents and grandparents would generally support me whenever there was a need for me to discipline one of their students. This was not always the case when there was a need for me to discipline a magnet student. In some instances, a magnet parent may challenge a decision I made, and threaten to see someone in a "higher" position.

I wanted desperately for the neighborhood students to believe they were capable of excelling. I presumed they might have felt somewhat resentful watching the magnet students enter the school, wearing their cute tutus, and music students carrying their instruments, which they owned, and didn't have to borrow from the school. There was very little exchange of conversation or acknowledgement between the magnet students and the neighborhood students. However, there was never, as I recall, any conflict or harsh words between the two groups. They seemed to have had a tacit understanding of respect toward each other. For this, I was thankful that I did not have to intercede in conflicts.

I had grown up in an environment much like the neighborhood students. The difference was that my high school was located where mostly white students resided. I was happy to see my friends when I went to school; however, I was not excited to attend many of my classes, where I generally was the only minority. I felt obliged to put on my smiley "mask" and remember my "mantra" when I engaged with my teachers or administrators. I also did not have the option to be bussed to a magnet school where I would have been able to take free dance and music classes.

I felt a surge of responsibility for the neighborhood students; a responsibility to encourage them and to show them that I genuinely cared about them. I acknowledged to students, that I was aware when they were absent, by saying such things as, "Kenneth, I missed you yesterday. I hope you are feeling better today." Even though I knew that the student had made a decision to not come to school. I made sure that I told the same student that I was happy that he was at school when I saw him several times after that.

Often, I felt guilty when black students told me they wanted to be rich like me. My success gave me the opportunity to live in a posh neighborhood and drive a prestigious car; although I did not consider myself rich. On the other hand, I believed it important that the neighborhood students understand that I worked hard and stayed focused. I earned my success. However, I did not want to discourage them by telling them that it was not an easy journey. I hoped their dreams would become a reality, just as mine had. I remember dreaming of wanting to have a big house with a freezer full of pizzas. I carried this image with me each time I left work with Mama, looking back at the big houses she cleaned. I didn't clamor to have a freezer full of pizza's, but I did achieve living in a big house.

Unless I was in a private meeting, I kept my door open so students would feel welcome to come in and visit. Often they would stick their head in and wave or give me a nod, as if to check to see if I was at school. When I was out of the office, even for a day, several students would stop in and inquire, "Where were you yesterday?" It felt good to be missed by my students, making me feel I was making a small difference in their lives. I believe I was their safety net. One day Kenneth, who preferred to be called Kenny, came in my office to see me during his lunch break. Kenny worked at being cool. His pants were hung low and he wore an oversized big shirt. He had a big beautiful smile, which he seldom displayed. I asked Kenny how he was doing in school and what his plans were for college. I often would ask the students this question, hoping to plant a seed. Kenny gave me a perplexed look, almost as though I had asked him a strange question. His response was, "There's plenty of ways to make money without going through all that." I surmised by his response that he wasn't doing well in school. I replied, "Kenny, you will feel good to know that you accomplished the goal of doing well and graduating from school, which may give you even more satisfaction than making money." Although Kenny respectfully listened to me, I am not sure he agreed with me. Still, each opportunity I had when I saw Kenny, I would continue to reinforce our conversation. When we passed each other in the hall, he would smile and give me "that look" as if to say, "I know. I didn't forget." I found myself having the same encouraging conversations with my students as Miss Grace had with me when I worked at Bishop Drum Nursing Home. Miss Grace would repeatedly inquire about my progress in school and my plans for going to college.

I never wanted to forget my beginnings, yet, ran to stay in the "race" to reach the goal line. It was very important for me to do everything I could to pass the torch forward to underrepresented students. For many of the students, there was a deep sense of hopelessness. The most overwhelming challenge for our counselors and me was assisting students and families in finding resources and support systems needed for daily survival, then following through by reminding them to keep appointments. Many families became overwhelmed and immobilized, feeling and believing "There are just too many obstacles to overcome." I was blessed to not have to worry whether there would be food to eat or if our family would need to move, several times, because of defaulting on our rent or home mortgage. It was very frustrating when white colleagues would ask me, "Why do these kids wear NIKE shoes when they are so poor?" It was a difficult question to answer because there was a lack of understanding, from those who queried, about why some parents who may have been single, unemployed, and were in poverty, yearned to want some semblance of being able to make their kids feel like they were like other kids, even if it meant not paying the rent. I came from a two-parent home, with both parents working, albeit making meager salaries. My parents didn't buy my sisters and me expensive shoes or clothes; however, I know they went "over the top" to buy us lots of toys and clothes for Christmas. I speculate that they put most of our gifts on credit cards, mainly Mama, in order to make the purchases. I recall overhearing some of the contentious discussions my parents had regarding money spent for Christmas presents. One might ask, "Why would your parents put themselves in debt for one day?" Their response might be, "Because it is important for us to make our kids feel jubilant on this very special day when they wake up on Christmas morning. It is our gift to us to see how happy our kids are when they open their gifts."

It saddens me when I see some of my former students standing on the corner looking aimlessly. However, it brightens my day when they acknowledge me with big smiles and hugs. The many students who graduated from college and are leading successful lives made me believe that there is hope for each and every student, regardless of some of their many challenges. I am blessed when they share with me that they were motivated because of my belief in them.

Wedged between Two Worlds

Things began to take a turn for the worse at the inner-city high school. Gang activity began to erupt throughout the community. The magnet program, which brought the school its prideful reputation, sizzled because fearful parents pulled their students out of the program. The district could no longer justify the bussing service offered to students throughout the district. Neighborhood parents taking advantage of open enrollment transferred their students to other schools in the district. Enrollment dropped dramatically. The remaining students were those who were not accepted to other district schools, many of whom were gang members attending the school, or students who were in the Special Education Program. There also were a few community parents who were dedicated to the neighborhood school who did not transfer their students and continued and wanted to see the school flourish. The school housed the largest Special Education Program in the district, giving the school even more of a negative perception. The negative perception that evolved gave me the impetus to stay committed to the students who remained. Each day was a challenge, not knowing what crisis might spew forth.

The junior high school where Erica attended in Lake Oswego was completely opposite. The students and parents were privileged. There was engaged parent involvement; many moms working in the volunteer room, wearing their tennis or golf skirts. Many of the parents and students had a sense of entitlement. Administrators were careful not to "step on toes," making it difficult for them to feel at ease to call parents when a problem arose. However, the school was not intimidated to call me. I received several calls regarding Erica's "bad" behavior, such behavior as not sitting up in her seat or being disrespectful by not saying "Good Morning" to a teacher. One of the calls I received was from the vice principal, informing me that Erica was being suspended. She requested that I immediately come and remove Erica from school. I was horrified believing that Erica had done something terribly wrong. When I inquired about the infraction, I was told, "Erica and her friend, Amy, continue to run down the handicap ramp after being told many times not to do so." My response was, "Why have I not been told this before?" The vice principal said, "We assume that the student would let their parent know that they had been warned when they are in trouble." I responded, "You must be kidding. A junior high school child is going to come home and report that they are in jeopardy of being suspended for running down a ramp." The vice principal answered, "Nevertheless, Erica must be picked up." I was upset that this act of defiance by Erica caused the problem and supported that Erica should have been disciplined. However, I was more furious that this was a problem that could not be handled by the vice principal. I could not believe the hostile words that flowed from my mouth. I said, "Are you serious by requesting that I drive from North Portland to Lake Oswego to pick up my daughter for running down a handicap ramp? Would this not have been an opportunity to use this as a teachable moment to teach the girls about having compassion, understanding and sensitivity toward students who have to use the ramp because of their disabilities?" She stopped me abruptly, by stating in a harsh tone; "I don't need *you* to educate me about when to use teachable moments. I have years more experience than you." At this point, I raised my voice, not believing how bitter I was feeling nor the words that came from my mouth. I responded, "Well, Miss Experienced Administrator, why don't we switch schools? Are you prepared to suspend a student who brought a loaded gun to school? I just appreciate that my students come to school safe and hope that they have a home to return to at night!" Being sarcastic, I continued, "It appears that your problems at this school *are much too* severe for you to handle!" I could feel that I had become much too furious and was allowing myself to get upset. I could hear it in her voice that she was becoming frightened, which made me feel worse. She uneasily responded, "I was told that you might be a difficult parent to speak with. I believe it would be more productive if you spoke with the principal about this situation regarding your daughter needing to be picked up from school. This conversation is going nowhere." She was absolutely right. There was no discernment about what I was trying to convey. I calmly told the vice principal that I would call my husband to pick up Erica. I didn't care what meetings he had, he was going to have to leave his job. I was not going to the school and have to look at the vice principal. Nor was I ready to deal with Erica. My emotions ran amuck. I was angry that we lived in Lake Oswego. I was filled with guilt that I allowed our daughters to be brought up in such an isolated bubble. I was even infuriated at Dan for not suggesting that we live in a more diverse part of the city when we were house hunting, even though I didn't suggest it to him. I was heartbroken that my students in North Portland did not have the same opportunities as the students in Lake Oswego. I was SO damn angry, hurt, and unhappy.

Months later, I received another "delightful" call from the junior high school. This time it was from the principal regarding another infraction by Erica. I was not surprised that the vice principal did not call me. It was the same day as the school's 8th-grade dance. I had taken Erica to Seattle to buy a dress for her to wear. An 8th-grade dance at Lake Oswego Junior High was a big deal. Parents bought their students designer dresses. Amy was not going to attend the dance. Erica was suspended because she and Amy were caught smoking, right outside the principal's office window. I said to my husband, "This is Erica's way of getting attention. She wanted to get caught! That way she would not have to go to the dance since Amy isn't going." Dan didn't agree with me, but being an educator for many years, I knew the signs of kids who were not happy and needed support. I talked to Erica, without scolding, attempting to get to the root of her behavior. She insisted things were going well, which I knew was not true. My instinct was telling me that, despite Erica's insistence that she was happy at school, there was a sad little girl who was insecure and trying her best to be accepted.

At the end of the semester, Erica brought her report card home. She received a D in her home economics class. When I confronted Erica, naturally, as most kids will respond, "I didn't know I had a D. The teacher did not tell me that." Even though I dreaded going to the school, I made an appointment to speak with her teacher. The teacher attempted to be cordial; I made sure I replied the same way. I politely inquired, "Why was I not told that Erica was doing poorly in class?" The teacher replied, smiling wryly, "I didn't know what Erica's grade was until I added up her points at the end of the semester." She continued to say, "The other parents stay on top of their students' progress." This comment implied that I did not. I didn't have the energy to invoke discord with another member of the faculty so I thanked her for her time and left the building. I was beginning to see a pattern, much like I experienced with Ali at the elementary school.

Dan and I came to the decision that Erica needed to be removed from the school as quickly as we removed Ali. We wanted to rescue Erica before she completely spiraled downward. I could see that it was even more difficult for Erica than it was for me to adapt to two different worlds. She was attending a majority-white school, lived in a white suburb, and was biracial. She was so vulnerable and fragile. She was too white to be black and too black to be white. We believe, to this day, that had we not removed her from the school when we did, she was on the road to destruction, academically, socially, and emotionally.

Erica was so angry when her father and I told her we were removing her from the junior high school. She had met several friends; however, the students she felt most comfortable with were the students who did not fit the mold of the majority of wealthy white students. The students Erica connected with best were students who were "down to earth", which were not considered in the same privileged class as some of the other students. They, like Erica, wanted to feel connected. I observed, in my personal and professional life, that there are two types of behaviors exhibited by underrepresented students. One, which I displayed, which was to overcompensate by doing well in school, become a "pleaser," and stay under the radar in order to not draw attention to myself. The other behavior; which Erica demonstrated, was to "act out," giving the impression that she didn't care what people thought of her. Taking Erica out of an environment where she was not being nurtured and was not flourishing was one of the best decisions we believe we made for her.

Erica became very successful. She graduated with a Master of Arts in teaching and became a science teacher both in Brooklyn and Los Angeles, teaching inner-city school students. She is currently a school administrator at a middle school in the heart of Los Angeles inner city. She has tremendous compassion for working with underrepresented students and families. She shared that her interactions with those with entitlement and wealth made her aware of those who do not share the same privileges. (Erica writes about her personal experiences, which is attached in the addendum.)

Both Erica and Ali adapted well at the private school. However, the distance from our home made it challenging for the girls to interact with their friends after school. Dan and I moved from Lake Oswego so our girls could be closer to their friends at Catlin, as well as, nearer to an urban setting where there were more diverse cultural events. When I moved from Lake Oswego, I did not leave with the most positive impression about the suburb. Ironically, a few years later, I was recruited to spearhead a private school for students challenged with Dyslexia, located in Lake Oswego. This position was the first time, in my working life that I was not conscientious about being hired as the first and only black person. I felt very confident and knew that I was hired because of my strong background and experience as a school administrator. I had already spearheaded two successful schools, prior to coming to this school. The few students of color, as well as their parents, seemed pleasantly surprised and happy when they met me for the first time. The students frequently stopped by my office before and after school. The founder of the school, Piper Park, and I had a great relationship. Piper was warm and caring and felt very compassionate about the students and the school. I loved working with her. I appreciated my great staff. The board members were also very supportive. I described this last position, before retiring from my educational career, as "my "heart job!" I had even begun spending more time, dining and shopping in Lake Oswego. I relished going to the little boutique stores and the quaint restaurants. In fact, I was sorry that I didn't take more advantage of the quaintness of the suburb while we lived in Lake Oswego. I was regretful that I had too harshly misjudged the small city.

Some of my black friends were aware that I was working in Lake Oswego. They cautioned me about driving to my job, fearing that I might be stopped by the police and questioned, without a cause. Not only did I "brush" these comments off. I reminded them that I had driven around Lake Oswego when I lived there. Other than having issues with the administrators and teachers at the two schools, where Erica and Ali attended, I had never encountered overt racial problems toward me. My black friends shared that Lake Oswego Police Officers, for no apparent reason, had pulled them over, several times. Fortunately, I never had any negative experiences with the Lake Oswego Police Officers.

However, my good fortune with the Lake Oswego Police, took a horrific downward spin. A humiliating event occurred between a white female police officer and myself, which caught me completely off-guard. I had just finished having lunch with two of my Bible Study friends; afterwards, I was walking underneath the parking structure toward my car. Just as I was getting into the car, a police officer, appeared out of nowhere on her motorcycle. She stopped right behind my car, preventing me from backing out. She bellowed resolutely, "Stay in your car, roll down your window, and hand over your driver's license!" I complied, but was both frightened and flabbergasted. I inquired, "What did I do?" She stated rudely, "You seem to be drunk. I watched you stagger to your car." I explained, emphatically, that I had absolutely nothing to drink and told her that I just had lunch with two friends. I insisted, "You can even check with the server," which she did not do, even though the restaurant was only 600 feet away. Before I knew it, two more police cars drove up behind the motor-cycle. I said to myself, "I can't believe this! She has actually called for back up!" I was wearing a business suit, tailored white blouse, and had on high heel shoes. I stood at 5'2". I didn't believe I looked like someone who was a threat. The two police officers walked over to me and requested that I get out of my car. I pleaded, "Please, I really have to get back to my school. Here, look at my business card." The card revealed my title, as Executive Director, and the name of the school. I continued, "I need to get to a parent meeting." I per-sisted, "I would never drink during working hours." I was inwardly so angry at having to continue to declare my innocence, but knew to keep my cool. One of the male officers remarked, "I need you to take a sobriety test before we can let you leave." The policeman told me to keep my head still and follow my eyes with a tiny flashlight he was holding. He moved the light back and forth. I was extremely nervous and was naturally not coordinated. I kept turn-ing my entire head following the light. The officer said, gruffly, "You are not supposed to turn your head. Keep it straight and just follow the light with your eyes." I said, "I am sorry I can't follow the light without turning my head." The officer had to chuckle at my inability to do this. I didn't think it was funny. He could see that I was anxious so he said, "Alright count to 20 backwards." Luckily I was able to comply with this request. I was almost in tears and em-barrassed. Several people were walking to their cars and staring at what was happening. I was worried that one of my student's parents might see me being interrogated, by not one, but three police officers, especially during the lunch hour. Finally, the police officer said to the other two, "I believe she's sober. Let her get back to her school." This was so surreal. One of the police officers followed me back to the school until I turned into the parking lot. I was totally shaking as I entered the building, but knew I had to quickly gain composure for the sake of the students and staff. However, I was emotionally unnerved.

Disappointedly, this grossly offensive act of racism awakened and re-minded me to stay vigilant and not be complacent. Being a professional woman, wearing a business suit and high heel shoes did not give me privileged rights. I was still black. Regardless of my status or how I was dressed, this type of treatment should not be an experience any person should encounter. My thoughts returned to what I had known to be true; racism, white privilege, power, and entitlement are the dominant factors that exercise control over people of color. I find it abhorrent to constantly be watchful. It's exhausting!

Intrinsic Self-Struggles

As I became more acquainted with people in the Portland area, I decided to become involved in nonprofit organizations. I was invited to sit on several community boards. I had become pretty well known because of my visibility as a school and district administrator. In addition, I became acquainted with parents who were philanthropists and whose children attended Catlin Gable, the prestigious private school where Erica and Ali attended. It was clear to me that one of the reasons for being invited to be a trustee on many community boards was an incentive for boards to advance their diversity and inclusion mission, which I thought necessary. In most instances, I was the only black trustee on many of the boards, which is still the case today. Very wealthy board members serve on these boards and are extremely generous donors.

I was neither wealthy nor considered myself privileged; however, I believed it was very important to have diverse perspectives and representation of minorities on these boards. As a trustee on the Catlin Gable Board, it gave me an opportunity to participate on the scholarship committee to review applications. I encouraged underrepresented students to apply to the school. I believed Catlin, with its exemplary academic program and small class sizes, would provide poor underserved students an opportunity to pursue an excellent education, which unfortunately many were not receiving in overcrowded and failing neighborhood schools. Some black folks criticized me for sending my girls to a private school, and for encouraging black parents to apply for scholarships. Their reason being, by doing so, I was not supporting minority neighborhood schools and draining poor schools of much-needed resources by lowering enrollment. Affluent families do not apologize for sending their children to safe schools with high expectations and standards. I did not feel that black parents should have to apologize for wanting the same high educational standards for their children, if the schools in their neighborhood were not exceptional high-performing schools.

I deemed it important to engage unrepresented populations in venues such as the art museum, theaters, ballet, and the symphony. I sat on each of these boards, not only for my own self-interest but to promote inclusion and engagement by and for minorities. I advocated for the art museum to provide free twice-a-year trips for underrepresented students to visit the museum and see works of famous artists. I yearned for students to have experiences that were not afforded to me when I was a child. I was elated that Jordan Schnitzer, a strong arts advocate and philanthropist, provided an opportunity for community members to attend, the Jordan Schnitzer Museum of Art at Portland State, for no charge. The museum gives underrepresented students and their families the privilege of exploring the arts, without having to be concerned about the cost.

I have relentlessly stayed engaged by volunteering for nonprofit organizations, especially in regard to education and health. I know the importance of staying connected in order to do my part in helping to create a healthier and better place to live. Foremost, it has been important for me to fight for justice and equality at every opportunity. However, I don't cherish sitting at the "table" as the "lone" voice, convincing others to join the battle. There will be insignificant change if there is not a unified voice—whites, blacks, and other minorities fighting for the rights for all. I have begun to shun accepting invitations to join boards that appear to draw only wealthy whites and inviting me as the "token" minority. I was chagrined when one of my white friends begged me to join a nonprofit organization where she sat as the chairperson of the board. She was openly honest with me and told me they were not receiving funding from local and federal foundations because there were no minorities represented on the board. Because of the organization's mission to provide necessary services to underrepresented children, I joined the board. In this case, it was about the children receiving services, not about me being irritated that I was the only black person on the board. It gave me an opportunity to become a strong advocate for underserved children. The boards that were crucial to me were ones whose focus was to heal oppression and injustice; ones that were inclusive, not exclusive; and, ones whose goal was to improve the lives of people, not by what they said but by their actions.

I began feeling more comfortable being the only black trustee. I viewed my presence as a way of opening doors for other minorities. I met many wonderful people whose frienships I continue to cherish. I found personal enjoyment and intrinsic value by accepting the invitation to serve. Admittedly, it still feels lonely at social events being the "only." What amazes me is when I share these feelings with my white associates; they truly do not understand my feeling of isolation. They actually are surprised and make comments like, "You are so popular. Everyone likes you." I continue to be "complimented" by the same remark, "You don't seem black. What makes you feel anxious?" It gets old! It becomes increasingly difficult to talk about tough issues regarding race because my white associates and friends sincerely can not grasp or understand the experience of being the only black person at all-white functions. I began to comprehend that this lack of understanding was a reality and, in most cases, were comments based on ignorance. By not being "too" black, it became easier, in some instances in order to adapt to their whiteness. I had learned to be versatile. Many blacks may feel differently and not believe in moving between two extremes. As for me, I experienced the benefit of being able to navigate both.

I have white friends who seem to be very comfortable being around black people; yet, I do not believe, or maybe it doesn't matter to them, that black people do not have the same entitlement as they do. Many whites do not discern there is a wide gap among whites and blacks, in regard to social injustices; their whiteness and privilege is taken for granted. Black people are aware of their blackness and how they are negatively perceived and judged based on the color of their skin.

Some of my black friends have become immobilized by the injustices of racism. The fight is just too difficult for them to overcome. They demonstrated their hurt by being angry and self-destructive. I have often thought that my way of conforming is just as self-destructive. It has taken a long time for me to realize the toll it has taken on me by trying to "dance" between two worlds. I have struggled very hard and given away much of "me" by wanting to escape poverty in order to have a better life. At times, I speculate that the price may have been too costly, based on my internal ire toward myself. Intrinsically, I was a scared young black woman who believed that it was more important to protect my parents from any detriment that would cause them shame or hardships with their employers than to speak up and protect myself. As many women, I experienced sexual abuse and harassment by white men in every job I worked, from high school throughout my career. Being black made me feel fearful to report these abuses for what I imagined may have had adverse consequences.

When I was young, my mother cleaned at a very large, prestigious white Congregation Presbyterian Church. My sisters and I took turns going with our mother to assist with cleaning. When it was my turn to go with Mama, my job was to clean the bathrooms. My mother would be in the other part of the church cleaning the pews. The Head Pastor, who was a very prominent white minister, would quietly come into the restroom and place his hands down my panties. I was so frightened. I didn't do or say anything. I hated the smell of his bad breath that he breathed on the back of my neck. I never told my mother because I was afraid she would lose her job if she said anything to the minister or told my father. I feared Daddy would have killed him if he knew what was happening to me. Mama died not ever knowing these sexual abuses occurred by the pastor of the church. A similar experience happened to me when I worked at a pathology laboratory while in high school. One of the pathologists would find me alone where I fed the rabbits (rabbits were used to detect pregnancy). He would place his arms around my breasts and kiss me grossly in the mouth. I stood frightened and never said a word, fearing it would cost me my job, which I desperately needed so I could save money for college.

There were countless other times that I endured these horrific encounters, too many to share. What I hated most was how I felt about myself. I continued to smile and talk to these predators, in front of others, as though nothing had happened. For many young black women, these experiences are much more intimidating; fearing they won't be believed and lose their job or bring shame to their families. I am mortified to admit that when it came to job opportunities, I had learned to become manipulative by being flirtatious and outgoing. The result of what I presumed would be beneficial in helping me move forward, in reality, gave me a sickly feeling of repugnance toward myself by opening the door to be preyed upon.

My warm and outgoing personality backfired when I interviewed for a vice principal position. The principal who interviewed me remarked, "You are too friendly and too cute to work in a school like this." He went on to comment, "A pretty little black girl like you wouldn't be able to handle the boys." I was a thirty-five-year-old woman and not a little black girl. I was angry and hurt. I was being perceived as too young, black, and inexperienced. Several of my white colleagues had already become principals by the age of 30. Most black teachers who aspired to become administrators were not given the opportunity until they were at least 40. Blacks, especially women, had to "go over and above" what was required to prove their competency. The majority of black men high school principals had previously been high school coaches. I realized I was still trying to walk the tightrope of not coming across too strong and black, nor too cute and overly friendly. I shared my job interview with a very "seasoned" black vice principal, Mrs. Bowman. She told me that she had applied year after year for a vice principal position. She was not offered a position until she was almost 50 years old. I solicited her sage advice on how I could be better prepared for a future interview. I was appalled by what she said to me. She was brutally frank! Her response was, "You need to stop being so demonstrably friendly toward white people, especially white men. They will never take you serious by the behaviors you exhibit! You need to come across much more serious and quit grinning so much!" Part of me was angry for the way she responded to me; another part of me appreciated her advice. My personal dilemma was that I am naturally friendly; smiling is an instinctive characteristic that I possess. This is the person I am. Looking stern and coming across very serious was something I had to work on. I needed to acquire a new image if I was to be looked upon as a viable candidate in the future. I worked at taking on a this facade. I became a principal at the age of 40 years old.

Mama

Blessings to Mama

My mother was so proud of my successes. When she came to visit, I would hear her talking to her friends on the phone…for hours. "You should see the beautiful home Paula and Dan live in. She has a big job, even though I don't quite know what she does. She just finished getting her Master's Degree." I was as proud of Mama as she was of me.

When my Mama died, it was one of the two saddest days of my life, the other being when Daddy died. I was devastated when Daddy died, but losing Mama was even more shattering. She had been alive to see me get married, to see both of her granddaughters be born, and experience my life as a grownup. I had become an adult orphan. My mother called me almost every morning at 5 A.M. She would always say, "Honey, did I wake you?" Then she would laugh and say that she forgot about the two-hour time change between Oregon and Iowa. Afterwards, she would call my sister, Judy, who lives in California, and say the same thing. Neither Judy nor I believed that Mama didn't remember the time differences. Mama just wanted to talk. We both continue to laugh about Mama's early-morning calls, however, I sorely miss her voice on the other end of the line.

Mama's outgoing, caring, and warm personality brought people to our home from all walks of life when she died, to offer their condolences. Many of my childhood friends, as well as my parents' friends, including people, who my parents worked for, came to our house. It seemed as though the entire black community came; some people I had never met, which was not surprising, since Mama made acquaintances with people wherever she went. My husband, Dan, came home with me to attend Mama's funeral. I knew the way most black folks celebrate the "passing of life" would be unfamiliar to Dan. To be honest, I was very nervous that he came, not knowing how comfortable he would feel. He was not used to being around a lot of black people and was appalled by the way people, nonstop, came in and out of our house, without knocking, laughing uproariously and hugging people they had not seen for a long time. The food and drinks kept flowing until all hours of the night. My face was covered with lipstick and sweat. I heard over and over, "Paula Marie, you sure enough are all grown up...look at you!" Then they would turn to Dan and say with big smiles, "And you must be Dan! Dorothea told us so many kind things about you." Mama adored Dan. I was uncomfortable, wondering what Dan was thinking, while experiencing a touch of "my world," He had never been among so many "down-to-earth" "let-it-all-hang-out" black folks.

It was apparent by Dan's constrained posture that he was out of his comfort zone. He was more at ease around middle-class black people, especially educated blacks in professional careers. I resented this side of him and disliked feeling self-conscious around my family and friends, knowing that he was judging them for being who they were. My friends were so outgoing and friendly toward him; he came off, what appeared to me, unapproachable. I found myself judging him, unfairly, for the way he was brought up in his culture and wanted desperately for him to accept my culture and the way I was raised. The difference was, it was not a necessity for him to move between two cultures. It was times like this that I questioned myself, "Why did I enter into an interracial marriage?" I reminded myself that there seemed few professional available black men when I married Dan; and, those who were single, dated white women. Although Dan and I came from divergent paths, I believed we would learn and respect each other. Our love would be based on the larger picture of the things we had in common that would keep us together. The funny stories shared about my mother by different friends were hilarious. It truly was a celebration. Dan, visibly, was not at ease observing the way my friends and family were memorializing my mother's death. When both Dan's parents died, people rang the doorbell, quickly paid their condolences in hushed voices, and left the house. No one came to Dan's home during all hours of the evening. Everything was very placid. There was serene background music during his parents' mourning that played throughout the day, before and after the funeral. Literally, one would know that someone had died. For me it was a rather gloomy feeling being at Dan's house during the time of his parents' death, very unlike the way our family celebrated my mother; we called it "Mama's Homecoming." Dan and I both had different opinions about what was a respectful way for honoring one's end of life. I have learned that many people do.

One of the most amusing memories of celebrating Mama's life was when my junior high school friend Norma Jean came to my home to pay her condolences. Norma Jean busted through the front door and ran over to me and yelled in the loudest voice, "Paula, I am so happy to see you! Girl, do you remember all those bitches I had to threaten to kick their butts because they were always picking on you during gym class?" She proceeded to tell the other visitors how mousy and scared I was of the girls in our gym class. Norma Jean continued to say to the guests, as she waved her arm and pointed her finger dramatically in the air, "I told ANY girl who said she was going to fight Paula Marie that she had to fight Norma Jean FIRST!" Everyone in the room was howling with laughter and clapping their hands clamorously. Dan seemed displeased, observing Norma Jean who, wanting to include Dan in the conversation, animatedly directed her stories toward him. Norma Jean was an impassioned woman. She was very tall and large boned. She had a very loud raucous voice and a thunderous laugh. Yet with all her imposingly bold demeanor, there was a restrained softness that I loved about her. Norma Jean really had not changed much in appearance, with the exception of having thinning short gray hair and a few missing front teeth. It was because of Norma Jean I found that some of the gruffest people have the most kindest and gentlest souls; most, I believe, are insecure and need others to be kind toward them. I always admired my mother for not judging people before getting to know them. I witnessed her becoming friends with some of the most bigoted people; her assumption was that, inherently, most people are good. I also have found this to be true, and made this my central premise when I first meet people, taking more time than just one encounter to know a person's heart.

After Mama's funeral, as I boarded the plane back to Oregon, I had ambivalent feelings leaving my hometown of Des Moines, Iowa. I began to recognize that I no longer had much in common with the people with whom I had grown up. Nevertheless, it still bothers me that I have lost some of my cultural ties and even some of my "blackness." I have respect for those who stayed connected to their roots. I never want to forget my beginnings, yet know I can never return to the past. However, having the experience and the ability to navigate between two cultures has been an asset. I knew the importance of being white enough to be accepted by whites; yet the importance of maintaining my blackness in order to hold on to my culture. Living in both worlds was essential in order to survive and prosper.

"For all our success in the professional world, we have paid a significant price in our private and emotional lives. A life of preordained singleness, by chance not by choice. A plight of alarming numbers for professional black women in America." —Anonymous

Further Musings

Reminisces of the effects of racism are still prevalent. I have come to grips, believing some things may never change. My heart sank when I heard the sad tone in my daughter Erica's voice when she called me, speaking almost inaudibly. I could hear by her voice that she sounded heartbroken. Erica told me that Tova, her three-year-old daughter, came home from preschool and said, sadly to Erica, "I am ugly, I hate my hair. I want to have pretty hair." Erica felt Tova's hurt. Erica told me that she had flashbacks on her own experiences as a child, not feeling as pretty as the white girls in her class. Erica also wanted to have long straight hair like the other little girls. Erica was devastated that Tova was having such unfavorable feelings about herself at such a young age. Erica shared, "Mom, I can't bear seeing Tova experience how I felt about myself when I was a child." Erica's comments evoked emotions that took me back to my memories about the negative feelings that haunted me, remembering the rude woman who snatched her little girl away from me and called me a "dirty little black nigger." I reflected back, "The effects of racism have impacted three generations in my family, the daughters and their mothers, from the same lineage, directly or indirectly." I asked myself, "How was it that Tova is already beginning to see herself in such a negative reflection? Did some innocent little girl comment about Tova's tight curls? Or did Tova observe for herself that she looked different from the other kids, sending her an implicit message that she was not pretty?" Tova was, indirectly, receiving the same perverse message that Erica received, and that I received; however, the messages Erica and I received were overt and cruel. Tova's thoughts about herself were coming from her own observations of looking different from the other little girls in her class. She was, subliminally receiving the message that looking different was not okay.

Hair texture, facial features, and skin color are the measuring perimeters of how not only some whites, but also how some blacks judge whether these characteristics are attractive or unattractive The majority of television anchorwomen are white and have long blonde hair. Women of color, in similar positions, wear long straight extensions in their hair. Seldom does one see a black anchorwoman with kinky hair. There is one black commentator whom I really admire. She has a short Afro, African-American features, and wears big earrings. She is an intelligent and reputable attorney. She speaks eloquently, with a black dialect. I have heard many refer to her as masculine, too black, too aggressive, and very negative. Many who listen to her may miss her tantalizing and interesting perspectives and viewpoints because they are focusing on her looks, which they may judge as distasteful. On the other hand, there is another anchorwoman, who is black has light skin and straight hair. This anchorwoman, understandably, is able to seamlessly become a chameleon in order to appeal to her white audience. I am not sure that either who are in the company of a mostly white environment are able to completely let their guard down. Interestingly, they either want to "prove" that they are comfortable with their blackness, by being on the defense, or they work hard to assimilate into the culture by adapting. Both ways create uneasiness and spurious behavior. I don't believe most whites understand the tension that constantly bubbles within blacks, when they are faced in certain uncomfortable situations. It still takes courage and "self-talk" for me to walk into some events where I am the only black and feel completely comfortable. My white friends show uneasiness when I share with them my "chameleon act". Many see me as a confident and self-assured person, who is comfortable around everyone. It has taken a lot of anxiety over the years to master this performance.

Advocating for Erica and Ali gave me more courage to speak up against injustice and inequity. I was going to do everything possible to prevent our daughters from being adversely impacted or be placed in perilous situations that may destroy their self-image or academic success. All rules of submissiveness were void when it was necessary for me to shield my children from harm. My memories of my mother reemerged about how courageous she was, as she pulled me over and placed her arms around my shoulder when the woman at Sears Department Store hurled ugly remarks at me. I also saw Mama's inner strength when she confronted Miss Lyons by telling her that I would be sitting with my black friends at the senior banquet. I learned from her, that when it comes to your children, you must stand up for what is right and just. Yet my mother became a proficient chameleon at making white people comfortable around her, knowing this was a survival tactic. I had been taught to do the same. This was a way of manipulating the "system," by exhibiting behaviors that aligned more with white norms, while not compromising my fundamental rights and principles.

Many would describe me as a very successful black woman. A woman who has achieved accomplishments in many areas: college graduate with a doctorate degree, an educator, a trustee on many prestigious boards, consultant, mentor, wife (for over 47 years), and mother of two professional adult children. One of my greatest honors was being inducted into my high school's Hall of Fame; important because it is my hope students of color will look up, as they walk to their classes, and view me as a role model. At the core of who I am is a woman who grew up in a community besieged with poverty, drugs, and despair. There were times when I became prey to other people of color. I felt exploited or pressured by being asked to do or support things that I was not willing to do. If I did not respond to what was asked of me, I was tacitly or boldly accused of thinking that I was better than they.

It depresses me when I return to my hometown in Des Moines, Iowa. It seems as though many of the adults I knew as a child got "frozen in a time capsule." Some of the females are raising their adult children's children, and in some cases the adult children are living with their mothers, in the same house where they were raised. Although I still maintain contact with some of the people who I grew up with, admittedly, our conversations are pretty limited to "Remember when we did…." Generally, other than us sharing things about our children or grandkids and the things we used to do when we were children, we don't have much more to talk about. When we encounter one another, I don't recall many of them inquiring or showing much interest in my career or what my life might be like. It's not that they may not care about my outside world; it's just that they are much more interested in having an interpersonal relationship with me than talking about my profession. My professional work has no context for them in which to relate. Many may not be able to visualize what life might be like, living outside of Des Moines, Iowa. I question myself, "Why I didn't I offer to share more about my current life, or to inquire about their lives and what was important to them?" Had I begun to look at their lives so bleak that I had become unaffected by their stagnant lives? If I am honest, I chose not to inquire, feeling it might have caused me irrational guilt about my success. I unrealistically convinced myself that I deserted those left behind. Although I still cherish the memories I shared when we were children, there are times when I don't know who the real "Paula" is. I have spent so many years delicately dancing between two worlds. On many occasions, I am unsure of which dance floor I am on. Yet I feel blessed that I am competent in being flexible enough to move, seamlessly, in and out of whichever culture I choose.

I may be considered to be wealthy by some of my Iowa friends who remained in Des Moines; ironically, my well-to-do white friends would barely consider me upper-middle class. Neither opinion makes any difference to me. I attend a church that prides itself on being multicultural, and has made a considerate effort to embrace and encourage all ethnic groups. The majority of the congregation is white. The church cannot be faulted for not having more blacks; few blacks live in the area where the church is located. Furthermore, I am not sure many blacks would attend; they enjoy and appreciate the cultural and social aspects of attending an African American church. Moreover, most people, black and white, chose to worship where they are most comfortable. It was difficult for me, at first, to attend a white church, after growing up my entire life attending a black Baptist church. There is not a title on either of the marquees stating the church is white or black: One knows by the congregants walking into the church. I still miss the gospel music and the high energy of the black church. Initially, I found myself struggling to enjoy what I consider "stuffy" white people's music. Presently, I no longer focus on the music, instead come to worship God and concentrate on the pastor's message.

Unfortunately, in today's local and national climate, we have become more racially divided than I can remember. The relationships among whites, blacks, and other minorities have become very acrimonious. It has become much harder to have healthy, rich, and courageous conversations about race and politics. One of my closest white friends and I seldom stay in contact with one another; our values and principals have shifted, making it difficult to integrate our individual perspectives because of our opposing viewpoints.

One of the positive outcomes that have come about as a result of the racial discord that is taking place in our society, is that many blacks have begun to take pride in wearing their hair "natural." On most television commercials and programs, blacks are shown wearing their hair in Afros, dreadlocks, or braids. Not too long ago, employers and school administrators would not have accepted this look as being professional; some students were suspended for wearing their hair in a style that unmasked their blackness. Lately, I observed Mrs. Obama sporting her "natural" hair, which I venture to say, would not have been an acceptable look for someone who was serving as the First Lady in the White House, even though she was of black origin. Interestingly, blacks wearing their hair in Afros, have experienced unwanted touching by some whites who want to feel their Afro. I always thought this to be an interesting phenomenon since I don't know of any blacks that are curious to feel a white person's hair. My hair stylist shared with me that when a white lady came up to her in the grocery store and asked if she could touch her hair; the stylist replied, "No! You are not in some petting zoo and I am not one of the animals!" She said the lady turned red and scurried out of the store. Although I applaud blacks that want to wear their hair, which depicts our heritage; I am comfortable wearing my hair how I choose. My hair does not define me.

As for me, I am relatively in a state of repose. I like the person I have become. The best word to describe me would be "content." None of my achievements have come without a price, including crying many tears of frustration, having bouts of loneliness, kissing butts, suffering from anxiety attacks, experiencing disappointments grappling with insecurities, losing trust, feeling fearful, retaining faith, maintaining resiliency, and fighting discrimination. It took me a long time to actually grasp the emotional, psychological, and physical toll it has taken on me, while perpetually doing a delicate dance, living white; being black. It has expended more energy than I can convey, proving to whites that I am an okay person. I was in a vulnerable position, adapting my personality to what I perceived made whites comfortable; however, not feeling comfortable with myself, by having to contort myself into someone I was not. It is difficult to elucidate to the oppressor what it is like to be oppressed. It has not been an easy journey, but one that has paid off in many ways, in reaching my attained goals.

I don't feel I have to apologize or feel ashamed that I have been successful. Does that mean that I don't feel compassion and will not continue to keep my arms open and my hands out to pull others behind me forward? No, I will never stop striving to help others experience success. I have had many cheerleaders and guides on my journey. My greatest cheerleaders were God, Mama, Daddy, Miss Grace, as well as, my daughters. However, I give my ultimate appreciation and gratefulness to Dan, my husband and paramount cheerleader, who has been my preeminent supporter and protector during all the years of our marriage. I surmise marrying a black woman in the 70s, may not have been an easy journey for him: although, not once did he ever share with me that it was difficult. His genuine and unconditional love for me did not allow others, who may not have agreed with his choice of marrying me, sway or intimidate him from listening to his heart.

My life has been composed of both a stormy and an exhilarating journey. I will continue to perform the "delicate dance." However, I envision there will be fewer and fewer dance steps that I will need to perfect. My resiliency is a result of personal courage. I find that I am beginning to dance boldly, to my own music, and am becoming pretty darn good at it!

Addendum

Little Mixed Girl

A Cultural Profile of Erica Kinney

From Whence I Came

My mother is Paula Marie Heariold born November of 1945 in Des Moines, Iowa to Deacon Frasier and Dorothea Brown. Both of their exact ethnicities are unknown although by societal measures, were considered African American. Dorothea was adopted at birth by Ezra and Cordelia Brown, an older African American couple. Neither her birth parents nor their ethnicities are known. Dorothea was very fair skinned so it is thought that she had quite a bit of Anglo blood, though she identified herself as an African American woman. Over the years, one of my mother's sisters has tried to uncover more about Dorothea's heritage. Each year it seems to change. It was once thought she was Syrian, then it changed to Sicilian and the latest is that she was half Jewish and half African American. My mother, Paula, claimed George Heariold, who is African American and Black Foot Indian, as her father since he adopted her when she was just six months old. Mom grew up in a three bedroom home with six sisters; some full, some half and others step. She was the only one to attend college and currently has her doctorate.

My father is Dan Larry Kinney born in July of 1941 in LaCrosse, Wisconsin to Don and Carol Kinney. As opposed to my mother's side, I can track my father's heritage as far back as the 1500s. His father is Norweigian and his mother is Norweigan and Swedish. My grandfather's grandfather, Niels

Opsahl was the first to come to the states in 1846. Supposedly he worked for a man by the name of Kinney and was often referred to as "Kinney's man" because people had difficulty with the correct pronounciation of his last name. Therefore, he changed his surname, and our name has been Kinney ever since. My grandmother's grandfather, Martin Gisvold was the first to come to the states in 1865. About six years ago, my uncle Jim contacted his distant cousins in Norway who still live on the Gisvold estate that has been in the family since at least 1790. My father and his siblings went to Norway to reunite with their cousins and stayed on the Gisvold farm. My sisters and I had an opportunity to visit later.

All of my father's siblings attended a four year college. His father was a high school principal for over forty years and his mother, a housewife. Both of my parents came from divergent backgrounds.

Childhood, the Formative Years

My parents and I moved from the Midwest to Lake Oswego, Oregon in 1977 when I was two years old. Lake Oswego at this time, if not now, was about 98% white. I really had no idea that I was different from the other kids until first grade. It was on the playground when one of the popular third grade boys pointed out in front of everyone that I looked like a "hamburger." I laughed it off with all the others but felt a thud sink inside of me. That night I went home and told my Mom who then explained to me that yes, I was different from the kids who I attended school with but reinforced that it was something to be proud of. However, no matter what she said to me that night, from there forward, I was mindful and self conscious of my difference. Other than my skin color, I was the same as these kids. We liked the same music, movies, toys and activities. I wasn't aware at this time that I was listening to "white" music and that I was talking "white." This came later. Therefore, it was difficult because I would for a moment feel the same as everyone and not be cognizant of my difference, when that invisible asterisk would pop up over my head again reminding me that I was. Black history month was the worst for me. Thank goodness February is the shortest month of the year! What was even better for me was that we usually only spent one or two weeks "celebrating" it. Anyhow, I would get stomach aches and hot flashes when we would read about or discuss topics such as slavery and Martin Luther King Jr. Anything that had to do with black people. I felt that the moment the textbook mentioned the word "black" or "African" the entire class would stop and look over at me. Of course this wasn't the case, but it sure felt that way. After all, wasn't I the minority delegate? It got to the point around fourth grade that I hated my Mom to come to the school. It again brought to attention that I wasn't like everyone else; kids with Moms who had fair skin and straight hair that smelled like fresh shampoo.

Many times throughout my childhood, I employed the laugh that I developed when that boy called me a hamburger. There were countless times in junior high and high school when racist jokes were told while I was present. There were the people that laughed, and then those that looked uncomfortable and would give a quick side glance to see my reaction. It was for this group I believe I used the laugh for most. It was almost as if I felt bad that they were feeling uncomfortable. Therefore, to ease their discomfort, "the laugh". The laugh that simultaneously came with the thud inside.

Off to College...

After graduating from high school in Portland, I attended the University of Washington in Seattle. I befriended three young women in the dorms with whom I later moved into an apartment. One was white, one Jewish and one African American. It was the most diverse group of friends I ever had up until that point in my life! For the first time, I was not the different one as we were all different from one another. I felt safe and welcomed in this group of friends. My race nor skin color was at the forefront of my identity any longer, but rather who I was as a person. This group grew to include more people of various ethnicities, sexualities and cultures. Unfortunately, this newfound social comfort put my academics on the backburner and needless to say, I did not excel by any means that year. Although I regret this, I do not regret the confidence that grew within me and my own growing self acceptance. I took some time off from school around my sophomore year and went on an excursion to Ecuador with a student group through UW; afterwards, I transferred to the University of Oregon to finish up my last two years of college. I couldn't quite figure out which direction in school I was going so decided to save my parents some money and attend one of the state schools. Being in

Eugene was interesting for me. I had a lot of friends from high school who attended U of O and I lived with a few of them. It was an awkward adjustment for me returning to the same people who knew me one way, and yet I felt like a different person. I didn't know how to be that same person they remembered while still maintaining my new acceptance and adoption of my developing "black side"… even apprehensive to play hip hop music that I now had an appreciation for while they were still listening to the "white music" we once enjoyed together. It never crossed my mind that nobody really cared and would even be open to new music as well as seeing me for the same core person that I was. I underestimated my friends.

…and Beyond

After college, I moved to Brooklyn where I remained for seven and a half years. I'm not sure how it really happened, but the majority of my social circle was African American. I believe it was to satiate my subconscious yearning to continue to connect with the other half of me. This is who I identified and felt most comfortable with. It was also my first time being surrounded by successful people of all colors. Most of my friends were lawyers, bankers, teachers, singers- the whole gamut. In New York, there was diversity within diversity! This was something I wasn't really exposed to in the Northwest.

As a child, I didn't want people to notice the added pigment in my skin; in New York, I became frustrated when people identified me as white. Ironically, I felt I didn't have enough pigmentation, I wanted to be darker! With age and experience, I finally started to come into my own, happy with my mixture of races. I feel that I can relate well to two races and identify with both.

I believe this to be a blessing for me as a teacher. The first school I worked in was predominately African American, most born and raised in Brooklyn. At the beginning of each school year, I think many of the students didn't quite know what to make of me. They couldn't figure out what race I was, I didn't have a Brooklyn accent or any accent for that matter and I was from Oregon (where's that?). I was able to relate to them as an African American; privy to the latest lingo, musicians and styles- but it was just as important to me that they knew I was white as well. That this person they grew to love (at times!), respect and trust was both like them (African American) and different from them (white.) In the latter case, I wanted them to see how they could still relate to and like someone different from themselves. In addition, I feel that being biracial is responsible for my very diverse interests and tastes. I enjoyed sharing these interests with my students and expanding on them whenever possible. The world we live in is becoming more and more of a "fruit salad," making it more colorful and rich. As a teacher, one of our sole responsibilities is to embrace and learn about these differences and teach children how to do the same.

What was once an immense internal and external struggle, now being an "oreo," as it was once put to me, is one of my favorite attributes.

Author's Note

While writing my memoir and recalling many of the unpleasant experiences I encountered as a result of racism; I began to question the "Why." I have been grappling with the "Why" about racism from the time I was a child. I found that the answer was simple; being black or brown gives the passageway for some whites to treat blacks and browns inequitably, disdainfully, and harmfully. The "Why" is the "just because" answer. Our parents responded with the "just because" answer when they really didn't have the answer to the "why." I continue to ponder the "Why?"

Why was I treated so unkindly by a white woman just because I wanted to be friends with the lady's little girl? Why did the white men, where my father worked, treat him so inhumane and make hurtful racial remarks toward him? Why did the white realtor tell my parents the house they wanted to buy was sold, when it remained on the market? Why did my parents tell my sisters and me that white people would accept us better if we acted and spoke the same way white people did? Why do white teachers have the liberty to decide whether a black student is capable of learning based on the teacher's deeply rooted cultural belief about the student's inability to learn? Why did I have to work much harder than my white colleagues to prove that I was as smart, knowing that I had no room for error? Why do some white people allow the mistreatments of the past influence their behavior toward blacks and brown people today?

Why do I have a frisson of hope that white people will begin to treat black and brown people with respect in a fair and evenhanded manner?

Why do I believe I will not experience this change in my lifetime?